# RUSSIAN
## in a week

Shirley Baldwin
and
Sarah Boas

# ACKNOWLEDGEMENTS

The authors and publishers are grateful to the following for supplying photographs: S. Baldwin, Barnaby's Picture Library, J. Allan Cash Ltd., J. Lowe, E. Mungall, Spectrum Colour Library.

ISBN 0 340 49425 5

First published 1989

Copyright © 1989 Shirley Baldwin and Sarah Boas

Typeset by Lasertext, Thomas Street, Stretford, Manchester.
Printed in Great Britain for Headway, a division of Hodder and Stoughton Publishers, Mill Road, Dunton Green, Sevenoaks, Kent by Richard Clay Ltd., Norwich.

# CONTENTS

# INTRODUCTION

**Russian in a Week** is a short course in Russian which will equip you to deal with everyday situations when you visit the Soviet Union: shopping, asking for directions, changing money, using the phone and so on.

The course is divided into 7 units, each corresponding to a day in the lives of the members of a school party and a cultural tour during their week in the Soviet Union. Each unit is based on a dialogue, which introduces the essential language items in context. Key phrases are highlighted in the dialogues, and the phrasebook section which follows lists these and other useful phrases and tells you what they are in English.

Within the units there are also short information sections in English on the topics covered, sections giving basic grammatical explanations, and a number of follow-up activities designed to be useful as well as fun. Answers can be checked in a key at the back of the book.

## BEFORE YOU LEAVE

One of the major problems facing visitors to the USSR is getting to grips with the Cyrillic alphabet. In fact, this is not nearly as difficult as it seems, and it is certainly worth spending some time making yourself familiar with it before setting out on your trip. If you do, you will be surprised at just how many road signs, street names, metro stations and so on you will be able to read.

### *The Russian Alphabet*

| Letter | Sound | Example |         | Letter | Sound | Example |                    |
|--------|-------|---------|---------|--------|-------|---------|--------------------|
| А а    | *a*   | as in *cat* |     | Р р    | *r*   | as in *rat* |                |
| Б б    | *b*   | as in *bat* |     | С с    | *s*   | as in *sand* |               |
| В в    | *v*   | as in *vet* |     | Т т    | *t*   | as in *tree* |               |
| Г г    | *g*   | as in *girl* |    | У у    | *oo*  | as in *shoot* |              |
| Д д    | *d*   | as in *dog* |     | Ф ф    | *f*   | as in *foot* |               |
| Е е    | *ye*  | as in *yet* |     | Х х    |       | sim. to *ch* in *loch* |      |
| Ё ё    | *yo*  | as in *yonder* |  | Ц ц    | *ts*  | as in *pets* |               |
| Ж ж    | *su*  | as in *pleasure* | | Ч ч    | *ch*  | as in *chap* |               |
| З з    | *z*   | as in *zoo* |     | Ш ш    | *sh*  | as in *shop* |               |
| И и    | *ee*  | as in *keep* |    | Щ щ    | *shch*| as in *fresh cheese* |       |
| Й й    | *y*   | as in *toy* |     | Ъ ъ*   |       | hard sign (not pron.) |       |
| К к    | *k*   | as in *king* |    | Ы ы    |       | sim. to *i* in *fit* |        |
| Л л    | *l*   | as in *bottle* |  | Ь ь*   |       | soft sign, see note |         |
| М м    | *m*   | as in *mat* |     | Э э    | *e*   | as in *bell* |               |
| Н н    | *n*   | as in *net* |     | Ю ю    | *you* | as in *youth* |              |
| О о    | *o*   | as in *for* |     | Я я    | *ya*  | as in *yarn* |               |
| П п    | *p*   | as in *pot* |     |        |       |         |                    |

**ай** is pronounced *eye*, **ей** is *yeah* and **ой** is pronounced *oi*.

* The hard sign (ъ) is not pronounced, but is sometimes found between a consonant and a vowel to indicate that these should be pronounced separately. The soft sign (ь) at the end of a word softens the preceding consonant, and produces a sound similar to a short *y* (as in *yet*).

## Pronunciation

1  Russian is a strongly stressed language, with stress always falling upon one syllable of a word (unfortunately, only experience will tell you which!). Vowels which are not stressed are pronounced slightly differently to vowels which carry the stress – they are spoken more quickly and tend to lose their value. Most notable is unstressed **o**, pronounced almost like an unstressed **a**: вода́/*va*da; unstressed **e** and **я** are pronounced almost like an **i**: теа́тр/*tiatr*.

2  You will see from the transliteration that some consonants at the end of words are pronounced slightly differently from the way in which they are written, e.g. хле**б** – хле**п** (bread).

3  R (**Р**) is rolled in Russian.

4  The transliteration used in this book follows the English sounds as far as possible. Note however that **kh** is the sound *ch* in *loch*, and **zh** is the sound *su* in *pleasure*.

## things to do

1  Some Russian letters are very similar to English. Look quickly at the alphabet and notice which letters look the same as or similar to English ones. Now see if you can read these words, and have a guess at their meaning:

| | | | | | |
|---|---|---|---|---|---|
| коме́та | да́ма | бале́т | такт | таба́к | котле́та |
| кафе́ | факт | ма́ма | фо́то | да́та | а́том |
| болт | ко́фе | балла́да | ко́ма | блок | каде́т |

2  Here are some more words in which all the letters are similar to English ones. See if you can read them (check in the key that you have pronounced them correctly):

| | | |
|---|---|---|
| да (yes) | дом (house) | де́ло (business) |
| кто (who) | как (how) | там (there) |
| э́то (this) | молоко́ (milk) | так (so) |
| те́ло (body) | мо́да (fashion) | ма́ло (little, few) |

3  These words all sound very similar to their English equivalents. Look at the alphabet and work out how to pronounce them (if you are right, you will also be able to say what they mean!):

| | | | | |
|---|---|---|---|---|
| такси́ | парк | кли́ник | фильм | во́дка |
| телефо́н | ви́за | буфе́т | банк | туале́т |
| вестибю́ль | тури́ст | дина́мо | метро́ | студе́нт |
| тра́ктор | центр | конце́рт | вино́ | газе́та |

## AT CUSTOMS

▶ ▶ ▶ **Arriving at the airport**    When arriving in the Soviet Union, you will need to pass through passport control and customs. Both of these can involve queues and delays, as officials are meticulous in scrutinising passport details and will often examine luggage very thoroughly. Have your passport, your visa and customs declaration handy – and make sure they have been returned to you before you move on.

### таможня/customs

Customs officials will not necessarily speak English, so listen out for these words:

| | | | | | |
|---|---|---|---|---|---|
| **деклара́ция** *diklaratsiya* | declaration | **па́спорт** *paspart* | passport | **ви́за** *viza* | visa |
| **заяви́ть** *zayavit* | to declare | **бага́ж** *bagazh* | luggage | | |
| **валю́та** *valyoota* | цурренцы | **чемода́н откры́ть** *chemadan atkryt* | open your case | | |

But probably the most important words you need to know are:

**да**/*da* yes **нет**/*nyet* no

▶▶▶ **Customs regulations** There are quite a number of items you're not allowed to bring into or take out of the country (for details, consult Intourist). Among the things you can't take in are hallucinatory drugs and narcotics, Soviet currency, goods carried for someone else, any kind of pornography, and books, films etc. which could be detrimental in any way to the interests of the Soviet Union. You can bring in and take out small quantities of wine, spirits and cigarettes, and the normal personal effects, travel goods and food for the journey. If your're thinking of taking more than two cameras, and such things as video-recording equipment, it's best to check first.

All foreign currency and cheques, jewellery and other valuables have to be registered on a customs declaration when you enter the country, and the form stamped. Be sure to keep your customs declaration safe throughout your stay so you won't be able to take your currency and valuables out again without it, and if you lose the declaration *it won't be replaced*. (If you're coming ashore from a cruise, you don't need to fill in a customs declaration.)

When leaving, you can bring out inexpensive souvenirs, jewellery, furs etc. bought in hard currency shops (keep the receipts), but among the things you can't bring out are Soviet currency, State loan certificates etc., works of art and antiques (such as icons, pictures, furniture, carpets, coins, books) of artistic, historic, cultural or scientific interest. These can only be exported with the permission of the Soviet Ministry of Culture and on payment of customs duty (equal to the full purchase price of the goods). Undeclared currency or other items are liable to confiscation, along with any vehicle in which they were hidden.

Note that you cannot bring **Soviet currency** into the country nor take it out, so if you change more roubles than you need you will have to change them back again and are likely to lose out on the deal. Most hotels used by foreigners as well as shops, bars and restaurants take hard currency, so it is advisable to change only a small amount of money into roubles and be prepared to spend it all. Note also that it is illegal to sell foreign currency to individuals.

## SAYING HELLO AND GOODBYE

After passing through customs, you will be met by the Intourist guide assigned to your group. If you are on your own, look for the Intourist desk where you will be given instructions about what transport has been arranged to take you to your hotel.

## приезд/the arrival

Mike Nash, a teacher of Russian, and his daughter Alice (16) arrive at Leningrad airport with a party of students at the beginning of a week's tour of the Soviet Union. They are greeted by their Soviet guide, Lena.

Lena: **Извините пожалуйста, вы мистер Наш?**
*Izvinitye, pazhalasta, vy mister Nash?*
Excuse me please, are you Mr Nash?

Mike: **Да, я.**
*Da, ya.*
Yes I am.

Lena: **Здравствуйте!** Я Лёна, ваш гид.
*Zdrastvuitye! Ya Lyena, vash geed.*
Hello, I'm Lena, your guide.

Mike: **Очень приятно.** Вот Алис, моя дочь.
*Ochen priyatna. Vot Alice, maya doch.*
Pleased to meet you. Here's Alice, my daughter.

Lena: Ах, это ваша дочь? **Доброе утро.**
*Ach, eta vasha doch? Dobraye utra.*
Ah, that's your daughter? Good morning.

Alice: **Доброе утро.**
*Dobraye utra.*
Good morning.

**Как вас зовут?** *What's your name?*

You will find that most people in the Soviet Union have three names, the middle one (patronymic) taken from the father's first name, e.g. Konstantín Pávlovich Ivanóv. Among Russians, the polite form of address is to use the first two names only. However, generally speaking you can call people you meet such as guides, waiters etc. by their first names. For business purposes, it is acceptable to use the terms **мистер/миссис/мисс** (Mr/Mrs/Miss) followed by the person's surname. You may also occasionally hear the words **господин/госпожа** (*gaspadin/gaspazha*) plus a surname for Mr/Mrs, as well as **товарищ**/*tavarisch* (comrade) or **коллега**/*kalyega* (colleague).

| | | |
|---|---|---|
| **Как вас зовут?** | *Kak vas zavoot?* | What's your name? |
| **Извините, вы ...?** | *Izvinitye, vy ...?* | Excuse me, are you ...? |
| **Да, я.** | *Da, ya.* | Yes, it's me. |
| **Я ...** | *Ya ...* | I'm ... |
| **Меня зовут ...** | *Minya zavoot ...* | My name is ... |
| **Я не ...** | *Ya ni ...* | I'm not ... |

| | | |
|---|---|---|
| **Как ваше имя/ ваша фамилия?** | *Kak vashe imya/ vasha familiya?* | What's your first name/ surname? |
| **Очень приятно** | *Ochen priyatna* | Pleased to meet you (lit. 'Very pleasant') |

## Greetings and farewells

You should always shake hands when introduced to someone in the Soviet Union, and you might like to say:

| | | |
|---|---|---|
| **Здравствуйте!** | *Zdrastvuitye* | Hello! |
| **Как вы поживаете?** | *Kak vy pazheevaetye* | How are you? |
| **Как дела?** | *Kak dyela* | How are things? |

To say 'Fine thank you', use the Russian word for 'good': **хорошо**/*kharasho*.

**Здравствуйте** is only used for the first time in the day you meet someone. After that you can say:

| | | |
|---|---|---|
| **Доброе утро** | *Dobraye utra* | Good morning |
| **Добрый день** | *Dobriy dyen* | Good afternoon |
| **Добрый вечер** | *Dobriy vyecher* | Good evening |

The Russian for 'goodbye' is **до свидания**/*da svidaniya*.

## Please and thank you

You will hear the Russian word for please, **пожалуйста**/*pazhalasta* a great deal as it also means 'pardon?' and 'don't mention it' (like the German 'bitte'). For 'thank you', say:

| | | |
|---|---|---|
| **Спасибо** | *Spaseeba* | Thank you* |
| **Спасибо большое** | *Spaseeba balshoye* | Thank you very much |

* Take care, it can also mean 'no thank you' when declining a request (simply add **да**/*da* or **нет**/*nyet* to make your meaning clear).

## BOOKING IN AT A HOTEL

▶ ▶ ▶ **Hotels**  The cheapest way to visit the Soviet Union is to join an organised trip, either through Intourist, or through one of the Soviet trade or educational organisations. However, it is possible to travel independently, and Intourist keeps a list of hotel rates in the major cities. Prices, which generally include breakfast and porterage, are not cheap for foreigners, and transfer from the airport or station is extra. You should book well ahead (hotels are particularly full from July to September when you may not find a single room) as only when booking is confirmed will you be issued with a visa. Accommodation is free for children under 2, and in some categories of room, children up to 12 pay only for meals.

You will have booked and paid for your hotel before leaving for the Soviet Union, and probably you won't know exactly which hotel you'll be staying at until you actually arrive at the airport. Accommodation can be in one of the following categories: Suite, De Luxe, First Class or Tourist Class. Many tours book visitors into First Class rooms with a bath or shower, WC and telephone. However, apartments with up to 4 rooms are available at some hotels, and the more expensive accommodation includes TV, radio, fridge and use of car and driver.

On arriving you should hand in your accommodation voucher (or your guide will attend to this) and you may be asked to fill in a registration form (**регистрацио́нный лист**/*registratsyonniy leest*) and hand over your passport, which will be returned to you later. After registering you will be given a hotel pass (**про́пуск**/*propusk*) or a card (**ка́рточка**/*kartachka*) which should be handed to the

**дежу́рная**/*dyezhurnaya* – the attendant (usually female) who keeps the keys on each floor of the hotel. In smaller hotels you collect your key directly from the desk, but in large hotels catering exclusively for foreign tourists, you will not be allowed past the entrance desk without first showing your pass.

▶ ▶ ▶ **Tipping** is officially discouraged and your hotel bill will include a service charge, but hotel staff, waiters, taxi-drivers etc. have come to regard a small tip of say 5% to 10% as normal.

## в гости́нице/at the hotel

The party transfers by coach to the hotel, where Mike speaks to the desk clerk.

Mike: **Здра́вствуйте. Меня́ зову́т Наш – вот мой па́спорт**.
*Zdrastvuitye. Minya zavoot Nash – vot moi paspart.*

Clerk: **Ми́стер Наш? … Но́мер два́дцать, на второ́м этаже́.**
*Mister Nash? … Nomir dvatsat, na ftarom etazhé.*

Mike: **На како́м этаже́?**
*Na kakom etazhé?*

Clerk: **На второ́м – вот ваш ключ.**
**Э́то ваш чемода́н? Лифт там …**
*Na ftarom – vot vash klyooch.*
*Eta vash chemadan? Lift tam …*

Mike: **Спаси́бо.**
*Spaseeba.*

Clerk: **Пожа́луйста.**
*Pazhalasta.*

| | |
|---|---|
| **Вот мой па́спорт/ваш ключ** | Here's my passport/your key |
| **на второ́м этаже́** | on the second floor |
| **Лифт там** | The lift's there |

*Asking about your room*

| | | |
|---|---|---|
| **Како́й но́мер?** | *Kakoi nomir* | Which room (number)? |
| **Но́мер два́дцать** | *Nomir dvatsat* | Room number 20 |
| **одина́рный но́мер** | *adinarniy nomir* | a single room |
| **двойно́й но́мер** | *dvoinoi nomir* | a double room |

**Но́мер с ва́нной/ду́шем/телефо́ном**
*Nomir s vannoy/dushem/tilifonam*
A room with a bath/shower/telephone

**Но́мер с телеви́зором/холоди́льником**
*Nomir s tiliveezaram/khaladilnikam*
A room with a TV/fridge

6

As well as keeping the keys, the **дежу́рная** will bring you cups of tea and run errands for you. If there is anything you need, you can try asking her to fetch it for you:

**Принеси́те мне пожа́луйста полоте́нце**  Bring me a towel, please
*Prinesitye mnye pazhalasta palatentse*
**... одея́ло, поду́шку, мы́ло**                    ... a blanket, a pillow, soap
*... adeyala, padushkoo, myla*

and when trying to find your way around, you can ask:
**Где**/*Gdye* Where ... ?

**Где туале́т/ва́нная/лифт?**  Where's the toilet/bathroom/lift?
*Gdye twalyet/vannaya/lift?*
**Где столо́вая/бар/буфе́т?**  Where's the dining-room/bar/buffet?
*Gdye stalovaya/bar/boofyet?*

Note that the voltage in most Soviet hotels is now 220 V.

## На како́м этаже́? *On what floor?*

It is important to be able to use numbers in Russian – then you will feel confident when changing money, shopping, asking for your hotel key, and so on:

| | | | | |
|---|---|---|---|---|
| 1 | **оди́н/одна́/одно́**\* *adin/adna/adno* | 11 | **оди́ннадцать** *adinatsat* |
| 2 | **два/две**\* *dva/dvye* | 12 | **двена́дцать** *dvinatsat* |
| 3 | **три** *tree* | 13 | **трина́дцать** *treenatsat* |
| 4 | **четы́ре** *chetirye* | 14 | **четы́рнадцать** *chetyrnatsat* |
| 5 | **пять** *pyat* | 15 | **пятна́дцать** *pitnatsat* |
| 6 | **шесть** *shest* | 16 | **шестна́дцать** *shisnatsat* |
| 7 | **семь** *syem* | 17 | **семна́дцать** *simnatsat* |
| 8 | **во́семь** *vosyem* | 18 | **восемна́дцать** *vasimnatsat* |
| 9 | **де́вять** *dyevyat* | 19 | **девятна́дцать** *divyatnatsat* |
| 10 | **де́сять** *dyesyat* | 20 | **два́дцать** *dvatsat* |

\*Note that the number 'one' varies according to whether the noun is masculine, feminine, or neuter – see grammar section. The number 'two' is **два** for masculine and neuter nouns, **две** for feminine nouns.

If you want to talk about which floor your room is on, you will need to know how to say first, second, third, etc.

| | | | |
|---|---|---|---|
| **на пе́рвом этаже́** | on the 1st | **на тре́тьем этаже́** | on the 3rd |
| *na pyervam etazhé* | floor | *na tryetim etazhé* | floor |
| **на второ́м этаже́** | on the 2nd | **на четвёртом этаже́** | on the 4th |
| *na ftarom etazhé* | floor | *na chetviortam etazhé* | floor |
| | | **на пя́том этаже́** | on the 5th |
| | | *na pyatom etazhé* | floor |

(Note that the first floor in Russian is the equivalent of the ground floor in England.) For a complete list of numbers, see p. 113.

▶ ▶ ▶ **Hotel services** If you are travelling with a group, the price of the tour will include transfer from the airport to the hotel, and porterage. Many of the large Intourist hotels offer the facilities seen in the illustration. You will be able to buy souvenirs, cards and stamps, newspapers and pharmaceuticals. At the service bureau, you can obtain information, arrange to go on excursions, book tickets for the theatre, concerts, ballet etc. and order a car. The bureau is generally open from 9 am to 9 pm.

| | |
|---|---|
| парикма́херская | hairdresser's |
| са́уна | sauna |
| апте́ка | chemist's |
| буфе́т | snack-bar |
| банк | bank |
| бар | bar |
| рестора́н | restaurant |
| бюро́ обслу́живания | service bureau |
| по́чта | post |
| кио́ск | kiosk |

## the way it works

### People and things (nouns)

The words for people and things in Russian are either masculine, feminine or neuter. Generally speaking, words ending in a consonant or **й** are masculine, those ending in **а**, **я**, or **ия** are feminine, and those ending in **о**, **е** or **ие** are neuter:

**па́спорт** (m.)
*paspart*
passport

**валю́та** (f.)
*valyoota*
(foreign) currency

**у́тро** (n.)
*utra*
morning

### My and your (possessive adjectives)

'My' and 'your' are adjectives, and in Russian adjectives have to agree with the noun they accompany:

| *masculine* | *feminine* | *neuter* |
|---|---|---|
| **мой** бага́ж | **моя́** су́мка | **моё** окно́ |
| *moi bagazh* | *maya sumka* | *mayo okno* |
| my luggage | my bag | my window |
| **ваш** чемода́н | **ва́ша** гости́ница | **ва́ше** одея́ло |
| *vash chemadan* | *vasha gastinitsa* | *vashe adeyala* |
| your case | your hotel | your blanket |

8

## I am, you are (the verb 'to be')

The verb 'to be' is generally omitted in Russian, so you would say:

| | | |
|---|---|---|
| **Я – ваш гид** | *Ya vash geed* | I am your guide |
| **Вы – мúстер Наш** | *Vy mister Nash* | You are Mr Nash |

To ask a question, simply use a questioning tone of voice:

| | | |
|---|---|---|
| **Вы мúстер Смит?** | *Vy mister Smeet?* | Are you Mr Smith? |

and to say no, you're not, use **не**/*ni*:

| | | |
|---|---|---|
| **Нет, я не мúстер Смит** | *Nyet, ya ni mister Smeet* | No, I'm not Mr Smith |

## Вот

**Вот** means 'here is' or 'there is'. Use it like this:

| | | |
|---|---|---|
| **Вот моя́ дочь*** | *Vot maya doch* | Here's/there's my daughter |
| **Вот мой пáспорт** | *Vot moy paspart* | Here's my passport |
| **Вот ваш ключ** | *Vot vash klyooch* | Here's your key |

* A large number of words ending in a soft sign (**ь**) are feminine.

# things to do

**1.1** **Pronunciation practice** These are some of the signs you may come across in the Soviet Union, perhaps at your hotel. See if you can pronounce them (look at the Key to see if you were right!)

| | |
|---|---|
| 1 РЕСТОРÁН | 2 ИНТУРИ́СТ |
| 3 СУВЕНИ́РЫ | 4 КÁССА |

They mean souvenirs, restaurant, cash desk and Intourist. Can you guess which one is which?

**1.2** See if you can greet the following people in Russian:

1 Your guide Tamara: say hello, and that you're pleased to meet her.
2 The lady attendant on your corridor: say good afternoon.
3 The hotel receptionist: say good morning.
4 A fellow-guest you have had a drink with: say goodbye.

**1.3**  A rather harassed guide is trying to round up a group of visitors. How do they answer his questions? (The first one is done for you.)

1  **Извини́те пожа́луйста, вы ми́стер Наш?**   (James Green)
   **Нет, я ми́стер Грин.**
2  **Извини́те пожа́луйста, вы ми́стер Наш?**   (Mike Nash)
3  **Извини́те пожа́луйста, вас зову́т Кларк?**   (Pat Clarke)
4  **И вас зову́т То́мас?**                       (Paul Thompson)
5  You are Anna Black – tell the guide your own name.

**1.4**  You and a friend are holding a conversation with the **дежу́рная** on your corridor:

1  First you want the keys for rooms 305, 308 and 310. What numbers do you ask for? (Note that in large hotels, you can get away with using the last two numbers only.)
2  Next you want to know where the bathroom is. What do you say?
3  There doesn't seem to be a towel in your room. What do you ask for?

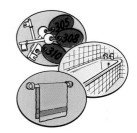

**1.5**  You are looking for the hotel bar, and overhear someone explaining where everything is. Can you tell which floor the bar is on? (**Нахо́дится**/*nakhoditsa* means 'to be found/situated'):

Буфе́т нахо́дится на двена́дцатом этаже́
Бюро́ обслу́живания нахо́дится на четвёртом этаже́
Бар нахо́дится на пе́рвом этаже́
Столо́вая нахо́дится на тре́тьем этаже́

According to the instructions, what is there on the twelfth floor?

# ORDERING DRINKS

Most hotels have a bar (**бар**/*bar*) in which you can use foreign currency to buy drinks. Larger ones also have a restaurant (**ресторáн**/*ristaran*) and a buffet or snack-bar (**буфéт**/*boofyet*) where you can get hot and cold drinks and snacks. The snack bar is often self-service, and food such as bread, cold meat, cheese, cucumber, etc., is sold by weight.

**Coffee** is normally black and rather strong. **Tea** comes without milk though in large hotels it may be served with lemon. If you want milk, you will have to ask for it. You may also find your tea has been pre-sweetened. There is a variety of syrupy carbonated drinks available in the Soviet Union. It is best to avoid these, and go for mineral water (**минерáльная водá**/*mineralnaya vada*) or fruit juice (**фруктóвый сок**/*fruktoviy sok*).

## в буфете/at the buffet

Lucy Brown, a journalist, is on a cultural visit to the Soviet Union. After spending the morning sightseeing, she goes back to the hotel for a drink along with Vadim, the Soviet guide attached to her group. Lucy knows some Russian, and is anxious to practice it.

Vadim:  (Shouts to the waitress) **Дéвушка! Дáйте чай, пожáлуйста.** (To Lucy) **Что вы хотúте?**
*Dyevushka! Daitye chai, pazhalasta. Shto vy khatitye?*

| Lucy: | **Ко́фе – с молоко́м.** |
| --- | --- |
| | *Kofi – s malakom.* |
| Waitress: | (Writing) **Чай, ча́шка ко́фе с молоко́м … Э́то всё?** |
| | *Chai, chashka kofi s malakom. Eta vsyo?* |
| Lucy: | **Да, э́то всё. Спаси́бо.** |
| | *Da, eta vsyo. Spaseeba.* |

Alice Nash and a friend arrive and sit down at a table.

| Waitress: | **Что вам уго́дно?** |
| --- | --- |
| | *Shto vam ugodna?* |
| Alice: | **У вас есть пе́пси-ко́ла?** |
| | *U vas yest pepsi-cola?* |
| Waitress: | **Нет, не́ту. У нас есть лимона́д и́ли фрукто́вый сок.** |
| | *Nyet, nyetoo. U nas yest limanat ili fruktoviy sok.* |
| Alice: | (cheekily) **А во́дка у вас есть?** |
| | *A vodka u vas yest?* |
| Waitress: | (sourly) **Нет, у нас во́дки сего́дня нет!** |
| | *Nyet, u nas vodki sivodnya nyet!* |

| **Да́йте чай** | Bring me some tea | | |
| --- | --- | --- | --- |
| **де́вушка** | waitress | **и/и́ли** | and/or |
| **Э́то всё?** | Is that all? | | |
| **у нас сего́дня во́дки нет** | we haven't any vodka today | | |

## *Asking for something to eat or drink*

| **Что вы хоти́те?** | *Shto vy khatitye?* | What do you want? |
| --- | --- | --- |
| **Что вам уго́дно?** | *Shto vam ugodna?* | What would you like? |
| **У вас есть пе́пси-кола?** | *U vas yest pepsi-cola?* | Have you got any pepsi-cola? |
| **У нас есть фрукто́вый сок** | *U nas yest fruktoviy sok* | We have fruit juice |
| **Нет, не́ту** | *Nyet, nyetoo* | No, we haven't any |

12

## Горячие напитки *hot drinks*

| | | |
|---|---|---|
| **Да́йте ко́фе** | *Daitye kofi* | Bring me some coffee |
| **Ко́фе с молоко́м/ с са́харом** | *Kofi s malakom/ s saxharam* | Coffee with milk/sugar |
| **Чай с лимо́ном/ с мёдом** | *Chai s limonam/ s myodam* | Tea with lemon/honey |
| **Чай без са́хара** | *Chai byez saxhara* | Tea with no sugar |

## Холодные напитки *cold drinks*

| | | |
|---|---|---|
| **молоко́** | *malako* | milk |
| **лимона́д** | *limanat* | type of lemonade |
| **ба́йкал** | *baikal* | cola |
| **фа́нта** | *fanta* | fizzy orange |
| **минера́льная вода́** | *mineralnaya vada* | mineral water |
| **апельси́новый сок** | *apilseenaviy sok* | orange juice |
| **я́блочный сок** | *yablachniy sok* | apple juice |
| **вишнёвый сок** | *vishnyoviy sok* | cherry juice |
| **тома́тный сок** | *tamatniy sok* | tomato juice |

To say 'a cup of coffee', 'a glass of tea', 'a bottle of lemonade' use these expressions:

**ча́шка ко́фе**/*chashka kofi*
**стака́н ча́я**/*stakan chaya*
**буты́лка лимона́да**/*bootylka limanada*.

Of course, you'll need to ask how much it comes to:

13    **Ско́лько с меня́?**    *Skolka s minya?*    How much is that?

## the way it works

### 'The' and 'a' (definite and indefinite articles)

There are no articles in Russian, so **кóфе**/*kofi* can mean 'coffee', 'the coffee' or 'a coffee'.

### How to say: You have

The verb 'to have' is not generally used in Russian. Instead, you will hear the expression **у нас**/*u nas* (lit. in the possession of us) for 'we have' and **у вас**/*u vas* (lit. in the possession of you) for 'you have'.

### Минеральная вода, фруктовый сок *(adjectives)*

Adjectives in Russian change depending on the noun they accompany  With masculine nouns, adjectives end in **ый**, **ий** or **ой**:

| | | |
|---|---|---|
| нóв**ый** бар | *noviy bar* | a new bar |
| рýсск**ий** гид | *rooskiy geed* | a Russian guide |
| больш**óй** стакáн | *balshoy stakan* | a large glass |

With feminine nouns, adjectives generally end in **ая** (a few end in **яя**):

| | | |
|---|---|---|
| нóв**ая** чáшка | *novaya chashka* | new cup |
| сѝн**яя** бутѝлка | *sinyaya bootylka* | a blue bottle |

With neuter nouns, adjectives generally end in **ое** (a few end in **ее**):

| | | |
|---|---|---|
| нóв**ое** окнó | *novaye akno* | a new window |
| хорóш**ее** молокó | *xharosheye malako* | good milk |

Don't worry too much about these different endings. The main part of the word stays the same, and as long as you get this right, you will be able to make yourself understood!

## things to do

**1.6  Pronunciation practice**

| | | | |
|---|---|---|---|
| КОНТÓРА | office | МУЖСКÓЙ | gentlemen's toilets |
| ЗВОНÓК | service bell | ЖÉНСКИЙ | ladies' toilets |

**1.7**  You and your friends are feeling thirsty after an afternoon's sightseeing and go into a cafe.

1  Ask if they have tea with lemon.
2  Ask the waitress to bring you a coffee and an apple juice.
3  Now ask for a bottle of lemonade, and say thank you.

**1.8**  You and your family go into a buffet for a quick drink before going
out to the theatre. See if you can talk to the waiter (**официáнт**/
*afitseeant*) in Russian:

| | |
|---|---|
| Waiter: | **Здрáвствуйте. Что вам угóдно?** |
| You: | (Ask for a cup of coffee and a glass of tea.) |
| Waiter: | **Вы хотúте чай с сáхаром úли без сáхара?** |
| You: | (You want it without sugar.) |
| Waiter: | **Без сáхара? Хорошó. И что ещё?*** |
| You: | (Ask if there's any tomato juice.) |

| | |
|---|---|
| Waiter: | **Нет, к сожалéнию** (unfortunately). **А у нас есть вóдка. Хотúте вóдку?** |
| You: | (Say no thank you. Ask for a fruit juice.) |
| Waiter: | **Ну – кóфе, чай и сок. Это всё?** |
| You: | (Yes that's all. Now thank him.) |

15  ***что ещё?** *shto yisho?* anything else?

## ORDERING BREAKFAST

Breakfast is traditionally a fairly substantial meal, served between 8.00 and 10.00 am, and although some hotels have now moved over to the Continental breakfast of bread (**хлеб**/*khlyep*), rolls and jam (**бу́лочки с варе́ньем**/*boolachki s varenyem*), you may also have a choice of hot dishes, cold sliced meats and cheese. In an old-fashioned hotel you might find smoked fish (**ры́ба**/*ryba*) or pancakes/fritters with sour cream (**бли́нчики со смета́ной**/ *blinchiki sa smyetanoi*) or with cottage cheese (**с тво́рогом**/ *s tvoragam*). Milk products are very popular in the Soviet Union, and **кефи́р**/*kefir* (soured milk) is often served at breakfast. A similar drink is **ря́женка**/*ryazhenka*. Soured cream is the accompaniment to all kinds of dishes, from soups and stews to pancakes and fruit puddings.

In larger hotels, breakfast may be already laid out on the table, but if there is a choice of hot dishes you may have to ask for what you want.

## завтракать/having breakfast

Lucy Brown is having breakfast with Donald Forbes, a retired doctor who learned his Russian in the Air Force. They call the waiter.

| | |
|---|---|
| Lucy: | **Молодо́й челове́к!** |
| | *Maladoi chilavyek!* |
| Waiter: | **До́брое у́тро. Что вы хоти́те?** |
| | *Dobraye utra. Shto vy khatitye?* |
| Lucy: | **Я́йца есть?** |
| | *Yaitsa yest?* |

| Waiter: | Да, коне́чно – у нас омле́т, я́йца всмя́тку, яи́чница с ветчино́й … |
| | *Da, kanyeshna – u nas amlyet, yaitsa vsmyatku, yaichnitsa s vyetchinoi …* |
| Lucy: | **Я возьму́ омле́т.** |
| | *Ya vazmoo amlyet.* |
| Donald: | **Да́йте мне пожа́луйста** бли́нчики со смета́ной. |
| | *Daitye mnye pazhalasta blinchiki sa smyetanoi.* |
| Waiter: | К сожале́нию у нас бли́нчиков нет. Соси́ски есть, и́ли колбаса́. |
| | *K sazhalyeniyoo u nas blinchikav nyet. Sasiski yest, ili kalbasa.* |
| Donald: | Тогда́ я возьму́ соси́ски. |
| | *Tugda ya vazmoo sasiski.* |
| Waiter: | Сейча́с. Хоти́те чай и́ли ко́фе? |
| | *Syichas. Khatitye chai ili kofi?* |
| Donald & Lucy: | Ко́фе, пожа́луйста. |
| | *Kofi pazhalasta.* |

| **молодо́й челове́к!** | waiter! (lit. young man) |
| **сейча́с** | at once/straight away |
| **коне́чно** | of course |
| **тогда́** | then |
| **К сожале́нию у нас бли́нчиков нет** | Unfortunately we haven't any pancakes |

**Что вы хотите к завтраку?** *What do you want for breakfast?*

| **Я́йца есть?** | *Yaitsa yest?* | Are there any eggs? |
| **Сыр есть?** | *Syr yest?* | Is there any cheese? |
| **Ка́ша есть?** | *Kasha yest?* | Is there any porridge? |

**Есть омле́т, колбаса́, ветчина́**
*Yest amlyet, kalbasa, vyetchina*
**Есть яи́чница, я́йца всмя́тку/ вкруту́ю, соси́ски**
*Yest yaichnitsa, yaitsa vsmyatkoo/ vkrutuyoo, sasiski*

There's omelet, (salami-type) sausage, ham
There are fried eggs*, soft/hard boiled eggs, little sausages

**Я возьму блинчики со сметаной** — I'll have pancakes and sour cream
*Ya vazmoo blinchiki sa smyetanoi*

**Я возьму сосиски** — I'll have sausages
*Ya vazmoo sasiski*

**Дайте мне хлеб, масло, варенье** — Give me some bread, butter, jam
*Daitye mnye khlyep, masla, varenye*

**Дайте мне булочки с вареньем** — Give me some rolls and jam
*Daitye mnye boolachki s varenyem*

*Fried eggs usually come in pairs, and when served with ham may be rather like an omelet.

## Language difficulties

Lucy and Donald managed to understand the waiter, but if you are not following what's being said, try one of these:

**Повторите, пожалуйста** — *Paftaritye pazhalasta* — Please repeat that
**Говорите медленно** — *Gavaritye myedlinno* — Speak slowly
or simply ...
**Я не понимаю** — *Ya ni panimayoo* — I don't understand

# the way it works

## Is there?/There is

**Есть** is a very useful word in Russian. Apart from the infinitive, it is the only part of the verb 'to be' that is commonly used, and means 'there is .../there are .../have you any ...?' etc.

**Есть молоко?** — *Yest malako?* — Is there any milk?
**Да, есть** — *Da, yest* — Yes, there is
**Есть булочки?** — *Yest boolachki?* — Have you got any rolls?
**Да, есть** — *Da, yest* — Yes, we have

## Nouns in the plural

If you are talking about more than one thing, most Russian words take **ы** (or **и** after **г, к, х, ж, ч, ш,** and **щ**) as their endings:

| | | |
|---|---|---|
| омлет/*amlyet* | омлеты/*amlyety* | omelets |
| сардина/*sardina* | сардины/*sardiny* | sardines |
| сосиска/*sasiska* | сосиски/*sasiski* | sausages |
| булочка/*boolachka* | булочки/*boolachki* | rolls |

Neuter nouns ending in **o** take **a** in the plural:

| | | |
|---|---|---|
| яйцо/*yaitso* | яйца/*yaitsa* | eggs |

(those ending in **e** take **я** and those ending in **ие** take **ия**)
NB  The adjectives 'my' and 'your' in the plural are **мои**/*maee* and **ваши**/*vashi*.

*things to do*

**2.1**  Here is the breakfast menu at your hotel. You would like fruit juice, fried eggs, rolls with butter and jam, and coffee with milk. Which can you not have?

---

### ГОСТИНИЦА МЕТРОПОЛЬ
#### Доброе утро!

| | |
|---|---|
| омлет | булочки |
| сосиски | масло |
| колбаса | сыр |

*напитки*

| | |
|---|---|
| кефир | чай с лимоном |
| фруктовый сок | кофе чёрный |
| какао | кофе с молоком |

---

**2.2**  The waiter is taking orders for breakfast. Tell him what you'd like.

Waiter:  Доброе у́тро. Хоти́те яи́чницу, омле́т или соси́ски?
You:  (You'll have an omelet.)
Waiter:  Омле́т с сы́ром и́ли с ветчино́й?
You:  (A ham omelet.)
Waiter:  Хорошо́. И что вы хоти́те пить*, чай и́ли ко́фе?
You:  (You'll have tea.)

* (to drink)

## MAKING PURCHASES 1

▶▶▶ **Stalls and stands**   You can buy such things as snacks, drinks, newspapers and magazines without having to go into a shop. Automatic street vending machines dispense soft drinks, carbonated water (**газиро́вка**/*gazirofka*), beer (**пи́во**/*piva*), pepsi-cola, etc. and Kvass (**квас**) – a mildly alcoholic drink made from fermented black bread and malt – is sold from tanks in the street. In summer, Russian beer, which is light and refreshing, can be bought from beer stalls.

You will find stands selling pies (**пи́рожки**/*pirazhki*), pastries (**пиро́жные**/*pirozhnye*) and other snacks, and in Moscow a Russian/American pizza stall is in business. Ice cream (from stalls or ice cream parlours) is extremely popular both summer and winter alike, and there are many varieties to choose from.

You can buy cigarettes (**сигаре́ты**/*sigaryety*) and cigars (**сига́ры**/*sigary*) from a tobacco kiosk (**таба́к**/*tabac*). Russian-style cigarettes (**папиро́сы**/*papirosy*) are thick, very strong, and come complete with cardboard tubes. Newspaper stands sell newspapers, magazines, maps and guidebooks (look out for the sign **СОЮЗПЕЧАТЬ**). You'll probably only find the *Morning Star* on sale in street kiosks, though your hotel may have a copy of *The Times*.

## мороженое купить/buying an ice cream

Mike Nash and his party have been sightseeing, and have a free half
hour before returning to the hotel. Mike wants to find an English
paper, but Alice and two of her friends decide to buy some ice
creams. They go to an ice cream stall.

Alice:  **Ско́лько сто́ит моро́женое?**
*Skolka stoit marozhenaye?*

Vendor:  **Три́дцать и́ли пятьдеся́т копе́ек.**
*Tridsat ili pyatdisyat kapeyek.*

Alice:  **Три по три́дцать, пожа́луйста.**
*Tree po tridsat, pazhalasta.*

**Ско́лько сто́ит моро́женое**  How much does an ice cream cost?

## в газетном киоске/at the newspaper stand

Assistant:  **Вы что-нибу́дь хоти́те?**
*Vy shto-niboot khatitye?*

Mike:  **У вас есть англи́йская газе́та?**
*U vas yest angliskaya gazyeta?*

Assistant:  **О́чень жаль. Америка́нский журна́л есть.**
*Uchin zhal. Amerikanskiy zhurnal yest.*

Mike:  **Ско́лько он сто́ит?**
*Skolka on stoit?*

Assistant:  **Рубль три́дцать копе́ек.**
*Roobl tridsat kapeyek.*

Alice:  (running over) **Мне ну́жно купи́ть
ка́рту Ленингра́да.**
*Mnye nuzhna koopeet
kartoo Leningrada.*

Assistant:  **Вот ка́рта Ленингра́да. Она́ сто́ит два
рубля́ де́сять копе́ек.**
*Vot karta Leningrada. Ana stoit dva
rooblya dyesyat kapeyek.*

Alice:  **Ско́лько сто́ят откры́тки?**
*Skolka stoyat atkrytki?*

Assistant:  **Сто́ят три́дцать копе́ек.**
*Stoyat tridsat kapeyek.*

Alice:  **Да́йте мне пять**, пожа́луйста.
*Daitye mnye pyat, pazhalasta.*

**Вы что-нибу́дь хоти́те?**  Do you want something?

**О́чень жаль**  I'm very sorry

## How to buy something 1

When you want to buy something, you can say:

| | | |
|---|---|---|
| **У вас есть ...** | *U vas yest ...* | Have you got ... |
| **англи́йская газе́та?** | *angliskaya gazyeta?* | an English newspaper? |
| **Мне ну́жно купи́ть** | *Mnye nuzhna koopeet ...* | I need to buy ... |
| **Я хочу́ ...** | *Ya khachoo ...* | I want ... |
| **Я хоте́л бы ...** | *Ya khatyel by ...* | I'd like ... (for a man) |
| **Я хоте́ла бы ...** | *Ya khatyela by ...* | I'd like ... (for a woman) |
| **моро́женое** | *marozhenaye* | an ice cream |
| **америка́нский журна́л** | *amerikanskiy zhurnal* | an American magazine |
| **ка́рту Ленингра́да** | *kartoo Leningrada* | a map of Leningrad |
| **путеводи́тель** | *putivadeetyel* | a guidebook |

And when you want to know what something costs, say:

**Ско́лько сто́ит?**  *Skolka stoit?*  How much does it cost?

| | |
|---|---|
| **Журна́л сто́ит рубль три́дцать копе́ек** | The magazine costs 1 |
| *Zhurnal stoit roobl tridsat kapeyek* | rouble 30 kopecks |
| **Ка́рта сто́ит два рубля́ де́сять копе́ек** | The map costs 2 roubles |
| *Karta stoit dva rooblya dyesyat kapeyek* | 10 kopecks |
| **Откры́тки сто́ят три́дцать копе́ек** | The postcards cost |
| *Atkrytki stoyat tridsat kapeyek* | 30 kopecks |
| **Три по три́дцать, пожа́луйста** | Three at 30 (kopecks), |
| *Tree po tridsat, pazhalasta* | please |
| **Да́йте мне пять** | Give me five |
| *Daitye mnye pyat* | |

## the way it works

### I want to buy a map (the accusative case)

When a word is the object of a sentence, and that word is a feminine singular noun, the ending changes:

| | | |
|---|---|---|
| **ка́рта Ленингра́да** | *karta Leningrada* | a map of Leningrad |
| **Я хочу́ купи́ть ка́рту** | *Ya khachoo koopeet kartoo* | I want to buy *a map* |
| **англи́йская газе́та** | *angliskaya gazyeta* | an English newspaper |
| **Да́йте мне газе́ту** | *Daitye mnye gazyetoo* | Give me *a newspaper* |

Adjectives in the feminine singular change their endings from **ая**/*aya* or **яя**/*yaya* to **ую**/*uyoo* or **юю**/*yocyoo* in the accusative case:

| | |
|---|---|
| **Да́йте америка́нскую газе́ту, ру́сскую ка́рту** | Give me an American |
| *Daitye amerikanskuyoo gazyetoo, russkuyoo kartoo* | paper, a Russian map |

Again, don't worry about these endings too much at this stage, as you will be able to make yourself understood even if you don't get them quite right.

## things to do

**2.3**  Can you complete this conversation using the words in the box?
Only one word will fit into each of the gaps.

Клиент:     Добрый день. У вас есть ......... газета?
Газетчик:   Да. Таймс есть.
Клиент:     Сколько он ........?
Газетчик:   ...... двадцать ..........
Клиент:     Я хочу также купить английский ..........
Газетчик:   Очень жаль. А у нас есть ......... журнал – Тайм.
Клиент:     Дайте мне ......... Ленинграда.
Газетчик:   Карта по-русски или по-английски?
Клиент:     ........., спасибо.
Газетчик:   Два ........ десять копеек.

| | | |
|---|---|---|
| рубль | американский | английская |
| карту | стоит | рубля |
| журнал | копеек | по-русски |

You will find a translation of this dialogue in the key on p. 109.
Did you manage to understand it?

**2.4**  **Сколько стоит?** How much does it cost?

Practise your numbers by saying how much all these things cost,
e.g.

**американский журнап 1 р. 30 к.**

Стоит рубль тридцать копеек.

1     **карта 2 р. 25 к.**

2     **русская газета 1 р. 10 к.**

3     **мороженое 50 к.**

4     **путеводитель 2 р. 5 к.**

# EATING OUT

▶ ▶ ▶ **Meals** Lunch (**обéд**/*abyed*) is the main meal in the Soviet Union, and consists of 4 courses – hors d'oeuvre, soup, main course, sweet. It is usually served in hotels and restaurants from 11.30 am to 3.00 or 4.00 pm. Dinner (**ýжин**/*uzhin*) may also have 3 or 4 courses, but you may not be offered soup. It is generally eaten between 7.00 and 10.30 or 11.00 pm. If you are on a group tour, all your meals may have been arranged for you at your hotel. However, if you are travelling by yourself or have booked half-board, you will have a chance to eat out.

The various state-run cafes and snack bars are generally crowded, especially at the end of the working day, and in many of them you eat standing at a counter. A **столóвая**/*stalovaya* is the equivalent of a quick cafeteria, and a **буфéт**/*boofyet* is a self-service snack-bar. You may also come across a **пирожкóвая**/*pirazhkovaya* selling mainly pies, a pancake house (**блúнная**/*blinnaya*) or a **пельмéнная**/*pilmyennaya* specialising in dumplings. There are a few Western-style cafes in the major cities, but fast food is only just beginning to catch on in the Soviet Union.

The **кафé**/*cafe* is really more of a restaurant and serves full meals with drinks, whereas a **ресторáн**/*ristaran* is likely to be a smart restaurant where people might go to celebrate an occasion. There will probably be loud music and dancing. Many of the best restaurants are in the hotels reserved for foreigners, and some cater for residents only. They may accept Intourist meal vouchers (**обедéнные талóны**/*obidyenniye talony*) – but you will generally have to book in advance.

You will be expected to leave your coat and any bags in the cloakroom. You are not obliged to tip attendants or waiters as your bill will include a service charge, but most people like to leave a little extra. Most restaurants close at 11.00 or 11.30 at night.

## приятного аппетита/bon appétit

Lucy has arranged to interview Tonya, a friend of Vadim's and a rather flamboyant character, for an article she is writing. The three decide to eat out at a well-known restaurant where Vadim has booked a table.

Vadim: **Здра́вствуйте, я заказа́л стол – на три челове́ка.**
*Zdrastvuitye, ya zakazal stol – na tree chilavyeka.*

Waiter: **Хорошо́. Сюда́, пожа́луйста, сади́тесь.** (Handing the menu) **Вот меню́.**
*Xharasho. Syooda, pazhalasta, sadityes. Vot minyoo.*

Vadim: **Что вы порекоменду́ете сего́дня?**
*Shto vy porikamendooitye sivodnya?*

Waiter: **Ку́рица о́чень вку́сна, и́ли бефстро́ганов …**
*Kuritsa ochin vkoosna, ili befstroganof.*

Tonya: **О, я о́чень люблю́ бефстро́ганов … и шокола́дное мо́роженое про́сто преле́сть!**
*O, ya ochin looblyoo befstroganof … i shakaladnaye marozhenaye prosta prilyest!*

Lucy: **Я хоте́ла бы сельдь, и пото́м ку́рицу.**
*Ya khatyela by syeld, i patom kuritsoo.*

Vadim: **И я хочу́ сала́т из огурцо́в, и би́тки. Скажи́те, Лю́си, вы лю́бите бе́лое и́ли кра́сное вино́?**
*I ya khachoo salat iz agurtsov, i bitki. Skazhitye, Lucy, vy lyoobitye byelaye ili krasnaye vino?*

| Lucy: | **Бе́лое, пожа́луйста.** |
| | *Byelaye, pazhalasta.* |
| Tonya: | (interrupting) **О, я предпочита́ю кра́сное …** |
| | *O, ya predpachitayoo krasnaye …* |
| Vadim: | **Вы бу́дете сла́дкое?** |
| (to Lucy): | *Vy booditye sladkaye?* |
| Lucy: | **Спаси́бо, не хочу́.** |
| | *Spaseeba, ni khachoo.* |
| Waiter: | (Returning) **Ну, вы бу́дете зака́зывать?** |
| | *Noo, vy booditye zakazyvat?* |

| **пото́м** | then |
| **я о́чень люблю́** | I love/I'm very fond of |
| **скажи́те** | say, tell me |

---

## Ресторан Ленинградский
### ОБЕДЕННОЕ МЕНЮ

*Закуски* starters
сельдь herring
икра caviar
салат из огурцов cucumber salad

*Горячие блюда* hot dishes
курица жареная с картофелем
  roast chicken with potatoes
бефстроганов/битки с рисом
  beef stroganoff/meatballs with rice
осетрина в томате
  sturgeon in tomato sauce

*Супы* soups
щи cabbage soup/бульон с яйцом clear egg soup
солянка рыбная spicy veg.and fish soup
рассольник vegetable and kidney soup

*Сладкое* dessert
шоколадное мороженое
  chocolate ice cream
ромовая баба rum baba
кисель kissel (type of fruit jelly)

---

## В ресторане *At the restaurant*

If you have already booked a table, you can say:

| **Я заказа́л стол** | *Ya zakazal stol* | I have booked a table (man speaking) |
| **Я заказа́ла стол** | *ya zakazala stol* | I have booked a table (woman speaking) |

If you haven't, try:

| **Я хочу́ стол на два/три/четы́ре челове́ка** | I want a table for |
| *Ya khachoo stol na dva/tree/chetyre chilavyeka* | 2/3/4 people |
| **на пять челове́к**    *na pyat chilavyek* | for 5 people |
| **Э́то ме́сто за́нято?**    *Eta myesta zanyata?* | Is this place taken? |

The waiter will say:

| **Сюда́, пожа́луйста, сади́тесь** | This way, please, sit down |
| *Syooda, pazhalasta, sadityes* | |

or

| **Жаль, все ме́ста за́няты** | I'm sorry, we're full up (lit. all the places |
| *Zhal, vsye myesta zanyty* | are occupied) |

*You might like to ask the waiter:*

**Дáйте мне меню, пожáлуйста**
*Daitye mnye minyoo, pazhalasta*

**Что вы порекомендýете/сегóдня?**
*Shto vy porikamendooitye/sivodnya?*

**Принесúте нам бутúлку винá**
*Prinesitye nam bootylkoo vina*

**Ещё одúн/однá/однó ..., пожáлуйста**
*Yisho adin/adna/adno ..., pazhalasta*

**Бóльше ничегó**
*Bolshe nichevo*

**Где здесь туалéт?**
*Gdye zdyes twalyet?*

**Дáйте счёт, пожáлуйста**
*Daitye sshot, pazhalasta*

Give me the menu,
  please
What do you recommend
  today?
Bring us a bottle of wine

Another ..., please

Nothing else

Where is the toilet?

Bring the bill, please

*and the waiter might say:*

**Вы бýдете слáдкое/кóфе?**
*Vy booditye sladkaye/kofi?*

**Вы бýдете закáзывать?**
*Vy booditye zakazyvat?*

**Сейчáс принесý**
*Syichas prinesoo*

**К сожалéнию, éтого у нас сегóдня нет**
*K sazhalyeniyoo, etava u nas sivodnya nyet*

**Заплатúте в кáссу**
*Zaplatitye v kassoo*

Are you having a
  sweet/coffee?
Would you like to
  order?
I'll bring it at once

I'm sorry, it's off today

Pay at the cash desk

## Likes and dislikes

**Я óчень люблю бефстрóганов**
*Ya ochin looblyoo befstroganof*

**Это прóсто прелéсть!**
*Eta prosta prilyest!*

**Вы лю́бите бéлое úли крáсное винó?**
*Vy lyoobitye byelaye ili krasnaye vino?*

**Я предпочитáю крáсное**
*Ya predpachitayoo krasnaye*

**Это óчень вкýсно**
*Eta ochin vkoosna*

I love beef Stroganoff

It's simply delightful!

Do you like white or
  red wine?
I prefer red

It's very tasty

▶▶▶ **What to order**   The Soviet Union is not noted for its cooking, but there are still one or two good restaurants to be found. Starters are often filling, and the first course (**пéрвое**/*pyervaye*) can be the most interesting. Be sure to try the smoked or pickled fish, red or black caviare (**крáсная úли чёрная икрá**/*krasnaya ili chornaya ikra*) and pancakes (**блúны**/*bliny*). Another favourite is **столúчный салáт**/*stalichniy salat*, a salad of mixed vegetables in mayonnaise. Soups are also very good, and include varieties of the well-known borsch (**борщ**) – beetroot soup, usually containing pieces of meat and

other vegetables, shchi (**щи**) – cabbage soup, and salianka
(**соля́нка**) – a very filling spiced vegetable soup with either smoked
fish or meat. Fish dishes to try are those with sturgeon
(**осетри́на**/*asietrina*), pike-perch (**суда́к**/*sudak*) and salmon
(**сёмга**/*syomga* or **лососи́на**/*lasasina*).

Favourite meat dishes include of course Beef Stroganoff
(**бефстроганов**), goulash (**гуля́ш**), Chicken Pojarsky (**котле́ты
пожа́рские**), Chicken 'Tabaka' (**цыплёнок ''табака́''**/*tsyplyonok
tabaka*) – in which the chicken is split, flattened and roasted with
garlic, and Chicken Kiev (**котле́ты по-ки́евски**). Popular dishes on
Russian menus are kebabs (**шашлы́к**), schnitzel (**шни́цель**),
beefsteak (**бифште́кс**) and pilaff (**плов**/*plof*). Meat dishes generally
come with assorted vegetables (**гарни́р**/*garnir*). Ice creams and fruit
compote (**компо́т**) are the most common desserts, but there are also
various gateaux (**то́рты**/*torty*), pies (**пи́роги**/*piragi*) and puddings
(**пу́динги**/*poodingi*).

For a full list of food, see p. 114. See also the section on Shopping.

**За ваше здоровье!** *Your good health!*

You will want to try some Russian wine with your meal, and perhaps to
propose a few toasts, in the Russian fashion. Ask for a bottle of white, red or
rose wine – **буты́лку бе́лого/кра́сного/ро́зового вина́** (*bootylkoo
byelava/krasnava/rozovava vina*), and say whether you want it dry, sweet or
sparkling – **сухо́е/сла́дкое/шипу́чее** (*sukhoye/sladkaye/shipoocheye*).
Russians tend to prefer their wines sweet. You might also want one of the
following:

| | | |
|---|---|---|
| beer (dark/light) | **пи́во (чёрное/све́тлое)** | *piva (chornaye/svyetlaye)* |
| champagne | **шампа́нское** | *shampanskaye* |
| whisky | **ви́ски** | *viski* |
| cognac | **конья́к** | *kanyak* |
| gin and tonic | **джин с то́ником** | *dzhin s tonikam* |
| vodka | **во́дка** | *vodka* |
| liqueur | **ликёр** | *likyor* |

уксус

растительное масло

чаша

ложка

перец   соль

стакан

салфетка   вилка   нож

тарелка

## *the way it works*

### More nouns

Nouns ending in a soft sign can be either masculine or feminine:

**сельдь** (masc.)  herring    **форель** (fem.)  trout

These nouns drop the soft sign and take **и** in the plural: **сельди**.

### More about adjectives

Adjectives in the plural end in **ые** or **ие**:

| | | | |
|---|---|---|---|
| **холóдная закýска** | a cold appetiser | **холóдные закýски** | cold appetisers |
| *khalodnaya zakuska* | | *khalodnye zakuski* | |
| **горя́чее блю́до** | a hot dish | **горя́чие блю́да** | hot dishes |
| *garyacheye blyooda* | | *garyachiye blyooda* | |

When the adjective comes after a noun, the éndings **ый** etc., **ая**, **ое** and **ые** are shortened. For example **вкýсный** (tasty):

| | |
|---|---|
| **бефстрóганов вкýсен*** | *befstroganof fkoosen* |
| **кýрица вкýсна** | *koořitsa fkoosna* |
| **морóженое вкýсно** | *marozhenaye fkoosna* |
| **би́тки вкýсны** | *bitki fkoosny* |

* Note the insertion of **e** to make pronunciation easier.

The form ending in **o** is used all the time to mean 'it's ...', e.g.

| | | | |
|---|---|---|---|
| **жáрко** | it's hot | **хóлодно** | it's cold |
| *zharka* | | *kholadna* | |
| **великолéпно** | it's wonderful | **ужáсно** | it's awful |
| *velikalyepna* | | *uzhasna* | |

## Russian case endings and pronouns

You will probably have realised that the endings of many words vary depending on where the word comes in the sentence. This is because there are six different 'cases' in Russian. We have already met the accusative case, which is used when a word is the object of the sentence. The dative case is used when we would generally use the word 'to' in English, and also after certain prepositions.

This is how it works for the pronouns we have met so far:

| *nominative* | | | *accusative* | | | *dative* | | |
|---|---|---|---|---|---|---|---|---|
| I | **я** | *ya* | me | **меня** | *minya* | (to) me | **мне** | *mnye* |
| you | **вы** | *vy* | you | **вас** | *vas* | (to) you | **вам** | *vam* |
| we | **мы** | *my* | us | **нас** | *nas* | (to) us | **нам** | *nam* |

Here are some examples:

| I see you | **Я вижу вас**/*Ya vizhoo vas* |
|---|---|
| I give (to) you | **Я даю вам**/*Ya dayoo vam* |

## things to do

**2.5  Pronunciation practice** You may come across one of these when looking for somewhere to eat. Can you pronounce them?

| КАФЕ–МОРОЖЕНОЕ | ice-cream parlour |
|---|---|
| ШАШЛЫЧНАЯ | kebab house |
| ЗАКУСОЧНАЯ | snack bar |

**2.6**  Lucy is with a group of friends at a restaurant, and is the only person who speaks Russian. What does she order for everyone?

red caviare, lamb with rice, compote
cabbage soup, chicken Kiev, vanilla (**ванильное**) ice
tomato salad (**из помидоров**), goulash with potatoes, cheese
sturgeon, pork with mushrooms (**с грибами**), kissel

**2.7**  Now her friends would like some drinks, so Lucy asks the waiter for the following: a bottle of red wine, a bottle of white wine, a gin and tonic, a light beer, and a vodka.

## LONG-DISTANCE TRAVEL

▶▶▶ **Trains**   The Russian railways are very geared up to long-distance travel, and a long journey can be an exhilarating experience. Tourists transferring from one major city to another often make the journey overnight in a comfortable sleeper (**спа́льный вагóн**/*spalniy vagon*). This can have either two berths (more comfortable and more expensive) or more usually four, with men and women sharing the same compartment – men usually take a turn in the corridor while ladies are dressing or undressing! Your ticket will include bed linen, blankets and pillow. There is no first or second class, and the old 'hard' and 'soft' categories have now disappeared, along with the wooden seats. Compartments can be **междунарóдный**/*mizhdunarodniy* (international – the most comfortable), **купéйный**/*kupeiniy* (generally 4-berthed) or **óбщий**/*obshchiy* (general). **Плацка́ртный**/*platskartniy* is a cheaper seat in a reserved coach.

If you are travelling independently, be sure to book ahead, and if you are going to be travelling for several days, it's a good idea to take some food and drink with you. Most trains have a dining-car (**вагóн-рестора́н**/*vagon-ristaran*) and for a few kopecks, the corridor attendant (**проводни́к**/*pravadnik*) will bring round glasses of tea at regular intervals. She will also wake you at a specific time if asked.

## на поезде/on the train

The group with which Lucy is travelling has made the overnight journey from Leningrad, and is due to arrive in Moscow early in the morning. Lucy engages in conversation with a Russian lady in her compartment.

Passenger: **Извини́те пожа́луйста, мо́жно откры́ть окно́?**
*Izvinitye pazhalasta, mozhna atkryt akno?*

Lucy: (whispering) Пожа́луйста. Скажи́те, **в кото́ром часу́ по́езд прихо́дит в Москву́?**
*Pazhalasta. Skazhitye, v katoram chasoo poyizd prikhodit v Maskvoo?*

Passenger: Я не зна́ю то́чно … в семь часо́в, ду́маю.
*Ya ni znayoo tochna … v syem chasof, doomayoo.*

Lucy: Спаси́бо. Вы живёте в Москве́?
*Spaseeba. Vy zhivyotye v Maskve?*

Passenger: Нет, в Заго́рске. **Мне ну́жно де́лать переса́дку в Москве́. По́езд на Заго́рск отхо́дит в** полови́не деся́того. Заго́рск о́чень краси́вый го́род …
*Nyet, v Zagorski. Mnye nuzhna dyelat pirisatkoo v Maskve. Poyizd na Zagorsk atkhodit v palavinye disyatava. Zagorsk ochin krasiviy gorat …*

Male passenger: (grumbling) Прошу́ вас не беспоко́ить меня́. Ещё ра́но, то́лько пять часо́в утра́!
*Prashoo vas ni bespakoit minya. Yisho rana, tolka pyat chasof utra!*

| | |
|---|---|
| **мо́жно откры́ть окно́?** | can I open the window? |
| **я не зна́ю то́чно** | I don't know exactly |
| **ду́маю** | I think |
| **Вы живёте в Москве́?** | Do you live in Moscow? |
| **краси́вый го́род** | a beautiful town |
| **Прошу́ вас не беспоко́ить меня́** | Please (I ask you) don't disturb me |
| **Ещё ра́но, то́лько пять часо́в утра́** | It's still early, only 5 o'clock in the morning |

## *Asking about train times*

**В котóром часу́ ...? Когдá ...?**
*V katoram chasoo? Kugda?*

(At) what time ...? (lit. in what hour?) When ...?

**В котóром часу́ прихóдит пóезд в Москву́?**
*V katoram chaso prikhodit poyizd v Maskvoo?*

What time does the train arrive in Moscow?

**Когдá отхóдит пóезд на Загóрск?**
*Kudga atkhodit poyizd na Zagorsk?*

When does the train leave for Zagorsk?

**слéдующий пóезд/послéдний пóезд**
*sliduyooshiy poyizd/paslyedniy poyizd*

the next train/the last train

**в половúне деся́того**
*v palavini disyatava*

at half past nine

## В билетной кассе *At the ticket office*

**Скóлько стóит билéт в ...?**
*Skolka stoit bilyet v ...?*

How much is a ticket to ...?

**билéт тудá и обрáтно**
*bilyet tooda i abratna*

return ticket

**билéт в одúн конéц**
*bilyet v adin kanyets*

one-way/single ticket

**Мне ну́жно дéлать пересáдку?**
*Mnye nuzhna dyelat pirisatkoo?*

Do I need to change?

**Это прямóй пóезд**
*Eta pryamoi poyizd*

It's a direct train

**Бу́дет пересáдка в Харькóве**
*Boodyet pirisatka v Kharkovi.*

You have to change at Kharkov

**С какóй платфóрмы? – Платфóрма нóмер два**
*S kakoi platformy? – Platforma nomir dva.*

From which platform? – Platform no. 2

## На вокзале *At the station*

**ПРИБЫ́ТИЕ**
*pribytiye*

arrival

**ОТПРАВЛÉНИЕ**
*atpravlyeniye*

departure

**расписáние поездóв**
*raspisaniye payizdof*

train timetable

**спрáвочное бюрó**
*spravachnaye byooro*

information office

**зал ожидáния**
*zal azhidaniya*

waiting room

**кáмера хранéния багáжа**
*kamira khranyeniya bagazha*

left luggage office

**бюрó нахóдок**
*byooro nakhodak*

lost property office

## На поезде *On the train*

**Это место занято?**    *Eta myesta zanyata?*    Is this seat taken?
**Нет, это свободно**    *Nyet, eta svabodna*    No, it's free

**Место**/*myesta* is a seat on a train, and **спальное место**/*spalnoye myesta* is a place in a sleeping compartment. The word for compartment is **купе**/*coopay*. You may find yourself in a smoking compartment (**вагон для курящих**/*vagon dlya kuryashchikh*). If you want a non-smoking compartment, look for a **вагон для некурящих**/*vagon dlya nikuryashchikh* or the sign **не курить**/*ni kureet* (no smoking).

## Можно ...? *Can I/May I ...?*

This is a very useful word in Russian, and you use it when you want to ask someone's permission to do something. For example:

**Можно открыть окно?**      Can I open the window?
*Mozhna atkryt akno?*

**Можно закрыть дверь?**      Can I close the door?
*Mozhna zakryt dver?*
**Можно курить?**      Do you mind if I smoke?
*Mozhna kureet?*
**Можно включить радио?**      Can I turn on the radio?
*Mozhna fkloochit radeeo?*
**Можно выключить свет?**      Can I turn out the light?
*Mozhna vykloochit svyet?*

If the answer is 'no you can't', use **нельзя**/*nilzya*:

**Нельзя курить**    *Nilzya kureet*    You mustn't smoke

## Где вы живёте? *Where do you live?*

**Вы живёте в Москве?**      Do you live in Moscow? **НЕ КУРЯТ**
*Vy zhivyotye v Maskve?*
**Я живу в Загорске**      I live in Zagorsk
*Ya zhivoo v Zagorski*
**Вы живёте в Нью-Йорке?**      Do you live in New York?
*Vy zhivyotye v New Yorki?*
**Я живу в Лондоне**      I live in London
*Ya zhivoo v Londani*

See p. 112 for the full form of **жить**/*zhit* (to live).

## TELLING THE TIME

### Который час? *What's the time?*

When travelling by public transport, it's useful to be able to tell the time. In Russian, it works like this:

**час**
*chas* — it's 1 o'clock

**два/три/четыре часа́**
*dva/tree/chetirye chasa* — it's 2/3/4 o'clock

**пять часо́в**
*pyat chasof* — it's 5 o'clock

**де́сять мину́т шесто́го**
*dyesyat minoot shistova* — ten past five

**че́тверть шесто́го**
*chetvyert shistova* — quarter past five

**два́дцать пять мину́т шесто́го**
*dvatsat pyat minoot shistova* — twenty-five past five

**полови́на шесто́го**
*palavina shistova* — half past five

What you are saying literally is 'ten minutes of the sixth', 'a quarter of the sixth', 'half of the sixth', etc. Note that **шесто́го** is pronounced as though the **г** was a **в**; this is true for all words ending in **-ого/-его** (**тре́тий** takes the ending **-его**). After the half hour, the pattern changes, and you use **без**/*byez* (minus), and the cardinal number for the hour:

| | | |
|---|---|---|
| **без два́дцати шесть** | *byez dvatsati shest* | twenty to six |
| **без че́тверти шесть** | *byez chetvyerti shest* | quarter to six |
| **без пяти́ шесть** | *byez pyati shest* | five to six |
| **шесть часо́в** | *shest chasof* | six o'clock |
| **утра́/дня/ве́чера** | *utra/dnya/vyechera* | in the morning/afternoon/ evening |

For 'at', use **в**: **в шесть часо́в** at 6 o'clock.

For train times, opening and closing times of museums, shops, etc., the 24-hour clock is often used, so you may see

| | |
|---|---|
| 13.00 (or 13 ч.) | **трина́дцать часо́в** |
| 15.30 | **пятьна́дцать часо́в три́дцать мину́т** |

Don't worry if you can't cope with expressing the time yourself – just listen out for those numbers (minutes and hours). If you don't understand, ask the person to repeat it:

**Пожа́луйста, ещё раз** *Pazhalasta, yisho raz* Once more, please

If you still can't catch it, ask for it to be written down:

**Напиши́те, пожа́луйста** *Napishitye pazhalasta* Please write it down

## в аэропорту/at the airport

▶ ▶ ▶ **Air travel**  Owing to the long distances between cities in the Soviet Union, it is just as common to travel by air as by train, and fares are not expensive. Airports however can be extremely crowded and you may have to face long queues. Airports are often some way out of a town, with transfer by coach or car. Air hostesses hand out boiled sweets and give helpful pre-flight information – however this probably won't be English, and you may find that once the plane has taken off, the air hostess is no longer on board! There are no separate areas for non-smokers on board Soviet aeroplanes.

### The vocabulary of flying

**Когда отлетает первый самолёт в Москву?**
*Kugda atlitayet pyerviy samalyot v Maskvoo?*
**В семь часов**
*V syem chasof*

When is the first flight to Moscow?
At seven o'clock

**Это рейс номер сто тридцать в Киев?**
*Eta reiss nomir sto tridsat v Kiev?*

Is this flight number 130 to Kiev?

| | | |
|---|---|---|
| **стюардесса** | *stewardyessa* | air hostess |
| **регистрация багажа** | *rigistratsiya bagazha* | luggage check-in |
| **вход на посадку** | *vkhod na pasatkoo* | departure gate |
| **посадка** | *pasatka* | stopover, transit |

**АЭРОФЛОТ К ВАШИМ УСЛУГАМ!**
AEROFLOT AT YOUR SERVICE!

≈✈АЭРОФЛОТ

## the way it works

### Verbs and how they work

You have met quite a few Russian verbs now, in various forms. The ending **-ть** means 'to ...', e.g. **курить**/*kureet* (to smoke), **стоить**/*stoit* (to cost), **заказывать**/*zakazyvat* (to order). This part of the verb is called the infinitive. Here are two regular Russian verbs with all their endings, and the complete list of personal pronouns:

**понимать**/*panimat* to understand

| | | | |
|---|---|---|---|
| **я понимаю** | I understand | **мы понимаем** | we understand |
| *ya panimayoo* | | *my panimayem* | |
| **ты\* понимаешь** | you understand | **Вы понимаете** | you understand |
| *ty panimayesh* | | *vy panimayetye* | |
| **он понимает** | he/it understands | **они понимают** | they understand |
| *on panimayet* | | *ani panimayoot* | |
| **она понимает** | she/it understands | | |
| *ana panimayet* | | | |
| **оно понимает** | it understands | | |
| *ano panimayet* | | | |

\* **ты** is the familiar form of 'you', used when speaking to close friends, children and animals. You may hear it, but you aren't likely to need it.

**говори́ть**/*gavareet* to speak, say

| | | | |
|---|---|---|---|
| **я говорю́** | I speak | **мы говори́м** | we speak |
| *ya gavaryoo* | | *my gavarim* | |
| **ты говори́шь** | you speak | **Вы говори́те** | you speak |
| *ty gavarish* | | *vy gavaritye* | |
| **он, она́, оно́ говори́т** | he, she, it | **они́ говоря́т** | they speak |
| *on, ana, ano gavarit* | speaks | *ani gavaryat* | |

Quite a number of verbs follow these patterns, e.g. **де́лать**/*dyelat* (to do, make), **знать**/*znat* (to know), **покупа́ть**/*pakoopat* (to buy), **ду́мать**/*dumat* (to think), **чита́ть**/*chitat* (to read), **изуча́ть**/*izuchat* (to study, learn). Others follow similar patterns, but with variations. For a list of common Russian verbs, see p. 112.

## *I live in Moscow (the locative case)*

The locative case is so called because it's used when you're talking about the place where something is located. (It is also known as the 'prepositional', as it is only used after prepositions.) After **в**/*v* (in, at, to) or **на**/*na* (on, at, to) nouns take the locative endings. Most take the ending **е** (those ending in **-ия** and **-ие** change to **-ии**, and feminine nouns ending in a soft sign change to **-и**):

| | |
|---|---|
| **Заго́рск – краси́вый го́род** | Zagorsk is a lovely town |
| *Zagorsk krasiviy gorat* | |
| **Я живу́ в Заго́рске** | I live **in** Zagorsk |
| *Ya zhivoo v Zagorskye* | |
| **Москва́ – столи́ца Росси́и** | Moscow's the capital of Russia |
| *Maskva stalitsa Rassii* | |
| **Мы в Москве́** | We're **in** Moscow |
| *My v Maskve* | |

## *Verbs of motion*

If you are going *to* a place and there is movement involved, the prepositions **в** and **на** are followed by nouns in the accusative case (i.e. the ending **a** changes to **y** for feminine singular nouns):

| | |
|---|---|
| **По́езд прихо́дит в Москву́** | The train *arrives* in Moscow |
| **По́езд отхо́дит на Ленинград** | The train *leaves* for Leningrad |

## *things to do*

**3.1** **Pronunciation practice** Here are some signs you will see at the station, and in many other places in the Soviet Union. Can you pronounce them?

ВХОД (entrance)      ВЫ́ХОД (exit)
ЗАПАСНО́Й ВЫ́ХОД (emergency exit)
ВХО́ДА НЕТ (no entrance)      ВЫ́ХОДА НЕТ (no exit)

**3.2** You have an hour's wait before your train departs, and want to sit down. What do you look for?

1 ка́мера хране́ния
2 спа́льный ваго́н
3 зал ожида́ния
4 бюро́ нахо́док

**3.3** Tonya wants to get to Moscow. She asks the assistant in the information office to look at the timetable. Can you answer her questions?

То́ня спра́шивает:   В кото́ром часу́ отхо́дит пе́рвый по́езд на
(asks)            Москву́?
                  В кото́ром часу́ прихо́дит по́езд в Москву́?
                  Когда́ отхо́дит после́дний по́езд из (from)
                  Ленингра́да?
                  Э́то прямо́й по́езд, и́ли бу́дет переса́дка?

## РАСПИСАНИЕ ПОЕЗДОВ – ЛЕНИНГРАД-МОСКВА

| поезд номер | отправление | прибытие |
|---|---|---|
| 25 | 0.30 | 12·30 |
| 12 | 10.00 | 22.00 |
| 3 | 17.40 | 05.50 |

**3.4** **Счастли́вого пути́!**/*Shastlivava pooti!* (Have a good trip!)

You have made it to the train, and you're looking for a seat. Can you communicate with your fellow passengers?

You:        (Ask if this seat is taken)
Passenger:  **Нет, свобо́дно.**
You:        (It's very stuffy – ask if you can open the window)
Passenger:  **Пожа́луйста.**
You:        (You forgot to look at the timetable. Ask what time the train arrives in Kiev)
Passenger:  **В Ки́ев? Часо́в в оди́ннадцать.**
You:        (You're feeling hungry. Ask where the dining-car is)
Passenger:  **Э́то ря́дом!** (next door)

**3.5** **Кото́рый час?**   The Soviet Union stretches across more than one time zone. Can you say what time it is in different places? E.g.:

London 3.15      В Ло́ндоне, че́тверть четвёртого
Leningrad 6.15   В Ленингра́де, че́тверть седьмо́го

1 London: 12.30        Moscow: 3.30
2 Moscow: 11.15        Irkutsk: 16.15
3 New York: 5.00       Leningrad: 13.00
4 Yalta: 6.45          Tashkent: 8.45

## ASKING FOR DIRECTIONS

▶▶▶ **Out and about in Leningrad** There are many museums, churches and interesting places to see in Leningrad, the great northern city built on water. If you are staying here, be sure to visit the Peter and Paul Fortress, which stretches along the north bank of the River Nieva. Built by Peter the Great, founder of Leningrad, it contains the Peter and Paul Cathedral in which the tsar himself is buried. Across the river is **St Isaac's Cathedral** (**Исаакиевский собор**/*Isakievskiy sabor*), with its splendid golden dome, built in the style of St Peter's in Rome. Visitors can climb up to the top for a magnificent view across the city. Worth visiting also is the **Kazan Cathedral** (**Каза́нский собо́р**/*Kazanskiy sabor*), now the Museum of the History of Religion and Atheism.

The **Winter Palace** (**Зи́мний Дворе́ц**/*Zimniy Dvaryets*), well-known for its impressive green and white facade, was once the home of the tsars, but now houses the world famous **Hermitage Museum** (**Эрмита́ж**/*Ermitazh*), so vast you would need six months to do it justice. The museum is particularly notable for its collection of French Impressionist and post-Impressionist paintings, and the many works of Picasso. Other museums are the Russian Museum, the Lenin Museum and the Museum of Literary History.

## как пройти в …?/how do I get to …?

It is their last afternoon in Leningrad, and Mike Nash and the members of his party are scattered in various parts of the city.

Alice wants to get to Palace Square. She asks a passer-by for directions.

Alice:       **Извини́те пожа́луйста, где Дворцо́вая пло́щадь?**
             *Izvinitye pazhalasta, gdye Dvartsovaya ploshchad?*
Passerby:    **Э́то недалеко́. Иди́те пря́мо, пото́м напра́во.**
             *Eta nidalyeko. Iditye pryama, patom naprava.*

**недалеко́**  not far                    **напра́во**  (to the) right

Next, she is looking for the Hotel Astoria.

Alice:       **Как пройти́ в гости́ницу ʼАсто́рияʼ?**
             *Kak praeetee v gastinitsoo Astoriya?*
Passerby:    **Асто́рия? – вон там, на углу́!**
             *Astoriya? – von tam, na uglu!*

**на углу́**  on the corner

Meanwhile, Mike is trying to find the way to the Finland Station.

Mike:        **Как пройти́ на Финля́ндский вокза́л?**
             *Kak praeetee na Finlyandskiy vakzal?*
Passerby:    **Напра́во, зате́м нале́во. Вы сра́зу уви́дите его́, нале́во.**
             *Naprava, zatyem nalyeva. Vy srazoo uviditye yevo, nalyeva.*

**зате́м**  then    **нале́во**  (to the) left    **сра́зу**  at once, straight away

**Shopping and the arts**  Visitors to Leningrad should not miss taking a stroll down the **Nevsky Prospekt** (**Не́вский проспе́кт**), the city's most famous boulevard, with its many shops, churches, and cinemas. And for entertainment there's the **Kirov Theatre** (**Теа́тр и́мени Киро́ва**/*Tiatr imyeni Kirova*), home of the Kirov ballet, opera and orchestra companies. Leningrad also has its own ʼWhite Nightsʼ arts festival, which is held every year in the third week of June.

Alice decides to pay a visit to the 'Gastiniy Dvor', the famous department store on the Nevsky Prospekt. She shows a passer-by her map.

Alice: **Пожа́луйста, где нахо́дится** Гости́ный Двор?
*Pazhalasta, gdye nakhoditsa Gastiniy Dvor?*

Passerby: Мы здесь, Садо́вая у́лица, а Гости́ный Двор там. Иди́те пря́мо, пото́м нале́во.
*My zdyes, Sadovaya ulitsa, a Gastiniy Dvor tam. Iditye pryama, patom nalyeva.*

**Мы здесь, Садо́вая у́лица** We're here, Garden Street

It's getting late so Lena decides to take a taxi to the theatre.

Lena: **Мо́жно?** (she gets in)
*Mozhna?*

Driver: Ку́да вам?
*Kuda vam?*

Lena: **В теа́тр** и́мени Киро́ва –
**скоре́е.**
*V tiatr imyeni Kirova –
skaryeye.*

Driver: Хорошо́, пое́хали!
*Xharasho, payekhali!*

| | |
|---|---|
| **бы́стро** | quickly |
| **пое́хали!** | let's go! |

### Указания *Directions*

It's fairly straightforward asking for directions in Russian. You can just ask **Где …?** (Where's …?) – or you can say **Где нахо́дится …?** (Where's … situated?):

| | |
|---|---|
| **Где Дворцо́вая пло́щадь?** | Where's Palace Square? |
| *Gdye Dvartsovaya ploshchad?* | |
| **Где Эрмита́ж?** | Where's the Hermitage? |
| *Gdye Ermitazh?* | |
| **Где нахо́дится Гости́ный Двор?** | Where's Gastiniy Dvor? |
| *Gdye nakhoditsa Gastiniy Dvor?* | |
| **Где нахо́дится Исааки́евский собо́р?** | Where's St Isaac's Cathedral? |
| *Gdye nakhoditsa Isakievskiy sabor?* | |

**Как пройти́ в/на** means 'how do I get to' if you are going somewhere on foot:

| | |
|---|---|
| **Как пройти́ в гости́ницу 'Асто́рия'?** | How do I get to the Hotel |
| *Kak praeetee v gastinitsoo Astoriya?* | Astoria? |
| **Как пройти́ на Финля́ндский вокза́л?** | How do I get to the Finland |
| *Kak praeetee na Finlyandskiy vakzal?* | Station? |

If you need to use some form of transport, say **Как проéхать?**/*Kak prayexhat?* instead. Of course, you will need to be able to understand the reply. This is what you can expect to hear:

**Вот он/онá/онó**
*Vot on/ana/ano*
There it is

**Это (не) далекó**
*Eta (ni) dalyeko*
It's (not) far

**Идите прямо/обрáтно, потóм напрáво/налéво**
*Iditye pryama/abratna, patom naprava/nalyeva*
Go straight on/back, then right/left

**Вон там, на углý/напрóтив/рядом**
*Von tam, na uglu/naprotiv/ryadam*
It's over there, on the corner/opposite/ next door

**Вы срáзу увидите егó/её, налéво**
*Vy srazoo uviditye yevo/yeyo, nalyevo* .
You'll see it at once, on the left

**Кудá?** means 'Where to?'. If you decide to take a taxi, the driver might say:

**Кудá вам?**  *Kuda vam?*  Where do you want to go?

and you might reply:

**В теáтр имени Кирóва, скорéе!**   To the Kirov Theatre, and quickly!
*V tiatr imyeni Kirova, skaryeye!*


## Я идý в теáтр *I'm going to the theatre*

**Я идý в гостиницу 'Астóрия'**   I'm going to the Hotel Astoria
    **в теáтр имени Кирóва**       to the Kirov theatre
    **в ресторáн 'Нéва'**          to the Nieva restaurant
**Я идý на Нéвский проспéкт**   I'm going to the Nevsky Prospekt
    **на Финляндский вокзáл**      to the Finland Station
    **на Дворцóвую плóщадь**       to Palace Square


*the way it works*

*Let's go to ...*

The verb to use when going somewhere on foot is **идти***:

| | | | | |
|---|---|---|---|---|
| **я идý**/*ya idoo* | I go | **мы идём**/*my idyom* | we go |
| **ты идёшь**/*ty idyosh* | you go | **вы идёте**/*vy idyotye* | you go |
| **он/онá/онó идёт**/*on idyot* | he etc. goes | **они идýт**/*ani idoot* | they go |

* Note that a few verbs have infinitives ending in **-ти**.

If someone is telling you which way to go, you'll hear **Идите ...**/*Iditye* (You go ...), and if a suggestion is being made, it's **Пойдём (в ...)**/*Paeedyom v* (Let's go to ...). When your guide feels it's time to make a move, he or she might say **Пошли!**/*Pashli* (Let's go!), and if you're in a taxi or a coach, the driver will say **Поéхали!**/*Payexhali!*

CPEДА **WEDNESDAY**

## В *and* на

Both of these can mean 'to', and it's a question of knowing which to use. There were quite a few examples in the dialogues – here are some more:

**пойдём** ... Let's go ...

| | |
|---|---|
| **в кинó**/*v kino* | to the cinema |
| **в цирк**/*v tsirk* | to the circus |
| **в музéй**/*v muzei* | to the museum |
| **в кафé**/*v kafe* | to the cafe |
| **на стадиóн**/*na stadion* | to the stadium |
| **на пóчту**/*na pochtoo* | to the post |
| **на выставку**/*na vystavkoo* | to the exhibition |
| **на стáнцию метрó**/*na stantsiyoo mitro* | to the metro station |

## Егó *and* её

For 'him' or 'it' referring to a masculine or neuter noun in the accusative case, use **егó**/*yevo*; for 'her' or 'it' referring to a feminine noun, use **её**/*yeyo*:

| | |
|---|---|
| **Вот собóр – я вижу егó** | There's the cathedral – I see it |
| **Вот гостиница – я вижу её** | There's the hotel – I see it |
| **Вот Лéна – я óчень люблю её!** | There's Lena – I like her very much! |

**Егó** and **её** are also used for 'his' and 'her':

**егó рóдина**/*yevo rodina*  his country    **её гóрод**/*yeyo gorat*  her town

## things to do

**3.6** **Pronunciation practice**  You will see these street signs all over the Soviet Union. See if you can guess their English equivalents:

СТÓЙТЕ  ИДИТЕ  СТОП  ПЕРЕХÓД  БЕРЕГИ́СЬ АВТОМОБИЛЯ

**3.7** Finding your way around

(*a*)  You have a free afternoon and want to look round the town. Find different ways of asking how to get to

1  the cinema      2  the hotel      3  the stadium

(*b*)  You are standing outside the hotel on the map, and hear your Russian guide giving these directions to some tourists. Can you tell where each of them wants to go?

1  Идите прямо, налéво, потóм напрáво. Вы увидите егó напрáво.
2  Это недалекó. Идите напрáво, на Большóй проспéкт, и вы увидите её на углý.
3  Вон там, напрóтив, рядом с теáтром.

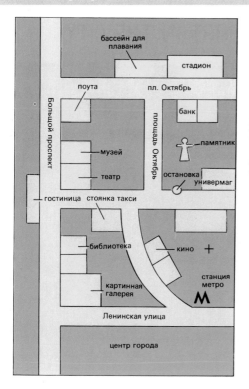

| банк | bank |
| бассе́йн для пла́вания | swimming pool |
| библиоте́ка | library |
| гости́ница | hotel |
| карти́нная галере́я | art gallery |
| кино́ | cinema |
| музе́й | museum |
| остано́вка | bus stop |
| по́чта | post office |
| собо́р | cathedral |
| стадио́н | stadium |
| ста́нция метро́ | metro station |
| теа́тр | theatre |
| универма́г | dept. store |
| центр го́рода | centre of town |
| це́рковь | church |
| у́лица | street |
| стоя́нка такси́ | taxi rank |

**3.8** You and various members of your group have asked the way to the Hotel Rossiya, the Chekhov Museum and Revolution Square, and you hope you have followed the directions correctly – but have you? Read the signs, and say where you actually ended up.

## TRANSPORT IN THE CITY

▶▶▶ **The Metro**  There are underground systems in Moscow, Leningrad, Kiev, Minsk and Tashkent, but the most famous one is in Moscow. Any visit to the capital is not complete without a trip on the Metro (indicated by the letter M, illuminated at night), with its fast, efficient service and its clean and beautifully decorated stations, many of which rival museums with their decor of marble, bronze, mosaics and glass. Visit **Площадь Революции**/*Ploshchad Revalyootsii* for its 'Heroes of the Revolution' – 40 pairs of bronze statues, **Комсомольская**/*Komsomolskaya* for its marble, mosaics and chandeliers, and **Новослободская**/*Novoslabodskaya* for its stained glass.

If you are to cope with travelling on the Metro, the main thing is to be able to decipher the names of stations (written of course in Cyrillic script). Exits, entrances, interchange stations and directions are well signed – but only in Russian. When you have spotted your station, see what colour line it's on, work out whether you need to change anywhere (**делать пересадку**) to get onto that line, and the rest is easy ... You pay a flat fare of 5 kopecks, which you slot into a machine at the top of the escalator. The red light changes, and you pass through the barrier – there are no tickets involved. If you don't have 5 kopecks, there are change machines (**Размéн**/*Razmyen*), and you can also change money at the **Кácca**. The name of every station, plus the one following it, is announced on arrival, so listen out for the stop you want. The Metro is open from 6.00 am to 1.00 am (5.00 am to 2.00 am on some public holidays), and there are fast trains every few minutes. It is best to avoid the rush hours (7.00 to 9.00 am and 4.00 to 6.30 pm).

## ПЕРЕХОД

## Алис едет на. метро/Alice takes the Metro

Mike and Alice Nash and the other members of their student group have also arrived in Moscow. Alice and her friend Sergei are keen to see the Metro, and break away from the rest.

Alice is looking for the station 'Sportivnaya', but can't locate it on her map. She asks for help.

Alice: **Извини́те, вы не зна́ете где ста́нция "Спорти́вная"?**
*Izvinitye, vy ni znayitye gdye stantsiya Spartivnaya?*

Traveller: **Вам ну́жна кра́сная ли́ния. Вот схéма Метрó – и вот Спорти́вная.**
*Vam nuzhna krasnaya liniya. Vot skhema mitro – i vot Spartivnaya.*

Alice: **Мне ну́жно дéлать пересáдку?**
*Mnye nuzhna dyelat pirisatkoo?*

Traveller: **Нет, вам не ну́жно.**
*Nyet, vam ni nuzhna.*

**вы не зна́ете где ...?**   do you know where ...?
**схéма Метрó**             plan of the metro

Sergei went in a different direction, and now he is trying to get back to the Prospekt Marksa. However, he isn't sure he's on the right train:

Sergei:
**Извини́те, э́тот по́езд идёт до ста́нции ''Проспе́кт Ма́ркса''?**
*Izvinitye, etat poyizd idyot do stantsii Praspekt Marksa?*

Traveller:
**Да, идёт.**
*Da, idyot.*

Sergei:
**Вы мне ска́жете, когда́ я до́лжен сходи́ть?**
*Vy mnye skazhitye, kugda ya dolzhen skhadit?*

Traveller:
**Това́рищ, Проспе́кт Ма́ркса – сле́дующая ста́нция!**
*Tavarish, Praspekt Marksa – slyeduyooshchaya stantsiya!*

**Вы мне ска́жете когда́ я до́лжен сходи́ть?**  Will you tell me when I have to get off?

**Я схожу́**/*Ya skhazhoo*  I'm getting off

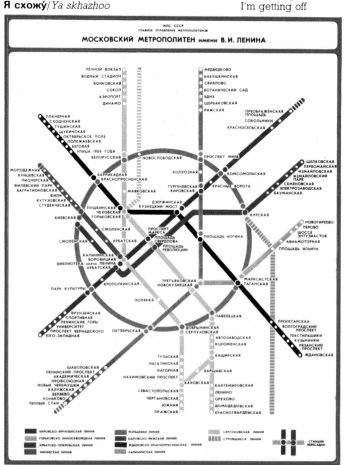

## Making enquiries

**Какой**/*kakoi* (what/which?) is a useful word when asking questions. It works like any other adjective:

**Какáя лúния для ...?**              Which line for ...?
*Kakaya liniya dlya ...?*
**Какáя слéдующая стáнция?**      What's the next station?
*Kakaya slyeduyooshchaya stantsiya?*

Note also:

| | | |
|---|---|---|
| **На какóй лúнии?** | *Na kakoi linii?* | On which line? |
| **На крáсной лúнии** | *Na krasnoi linii* | On the red line |
| **На калúнинской лúнии** | *Na kalininskoi linii* | On the Kalinin line |

**Этот пóезд идёт до стáнции "Проспéкт Мáркса"**   This train is going to
*Etat poyizd idyot do stantsii Praspekt Marksa*            Prospekt Marksa

When you're on the train, listen out for these announcements:

**Осторóжно, двéри закрывáются!**      Attention, doors closing!
*Astarozhna, dveri zakryvayootsa*
**Слéдующая – Проспéкт Мáркса**        Next stop Prospekt Marksa
*Slyeduyooshchaya – Praspekt Marksa*


## I need to, I must

You have already met the expression **нýжно**/*nuzhna*:

**Мне нýжно дéлать пересáдку? – Нет, вам не нýжно.**
Do I need to change?                – No, you don't need to.

A similar expression that you'll hear frequently is **вам нáдо**/*vam nada* meaning 'you ought to'. **Не нáдо**/*ni nada* on its own is often used with the meaning 'you don't have to' or simply 'don't!'.

**Дóлжен**/*dolzhen* means 'must' or 'have to', but is used in a more specific way. It is rather like a short adjective:

| | | | |
|---|---|---|---|
| Sergei: | **Я дóлжен сходúть** | *Ya dolzhen skhadit* | I have to get out |
| Alice: | **Я должнá сходúть** | *Ya dulzhna skhadit* | I have to get out |
| Traveller: | **Вы должнû сходúть** | *Vy dulzhny skhadit* | You must get out |


## Цвета/*Tsvyeta (Colours)*

It's useful to know your colours so you can check that you're on the right line:

| | | | | |
|---|---|---|---|---|
| black | **чёрный**/*chorniy* | | purple | **пурпýрный**/*purpurniy* |
| white | **бéлый**/*byeliy* | | mauve | **сирéневый**/*siryeneviy* |
| red | **крáсный**/*krasniy* | | orange | **орáнжевый**/*aranzheviy* |
| blue (dark) | **сúний**/*siniy* | | pink | **рóзовый**/*rozaviy* |
| (light) | **голубóй**/*galuboi* | | grey | **сéрый**/*syeriy* |
| green | **зелёный**/*zilyoniy* | | | |
| yellow | **жёлтый**/*zholtiy* | | dark | **темнó**/*tyemno* |
| brown | **корúчневый**/*karichnievi* | light | **светлó**/*svyetlo* |

▶▶▶ **Buses and trams**  If you're feeling really adventurous, you can try taking the bus (**автобус**/*aftoboos*), trolleybus (**троллейбус**/ *trallyeiboos*) or tram (**трамвай**/*tramvai*). A flat rate fare operates here too, but you put your money in a collecting box and tear a ticket from the roll hanging up. If you don't have the correct money, wait until you have got some change from another passenger before taking your ticket. If the bus is crowded, you will find people passing their fares along to the person nearest the box. Tickets should be validated at one of the stamping machines inside the bus. Both buses and trams run from very early in the morning (5.00 or 5.30 am to 1 am).

| | |
|---|---|
| **Где остановка автобуса?** *Gdye astanofka aftoboosa?* | Where's the bus stop? |
| **остановка троллейбуса/трамвая** *astanofka trallyeiboosa/tramvaya* | trolleybus/tram stop |
| **Вам нужно номер 12** *Vam nuzhna nomir dvyenatsat* | You need a number 12 |
| **В центр города, какой номер?** *V tsentr gorada, kakoi nomir?* | What number for the town centre? |

▶▶▶ **Taxis** can be found at taxi ranks (**стоянка такси**/*stayanka taksi*), recognisable by the sign of a large T, and can also be hailed in the street (though this is not always successful). Russian taxis have a checked stripe either along the side or on the roof, and an illuminated light in the windscreen or on the roof indicates that the taxi is free. All taxis are metered, and you do not pay anything extra for the number of passengers or for luggage. If you know in advance that you're going to need a taxi, ask your hotel service bureau to call one for you.

| | | |
|---|---|---|
| **На вокзал, спасибо** | *Na vakzal, spaseeba* | To the station please |
| **В аэропорт ...** | *V aeroport ...* | To the airport ... |
| **Я спешу!** | *Ya spishoo!* | I'm in a hurry! |

## MOTORING

▶▶ **Hiring a car** It is now possible to hire a car (**взять напрокáт машúну**/*vzyat naprakat mashinoo*) for driving around town or on recognised Intourist routes, though this facility only exists in a few major towns. In others, your car comes complete with a driver. Be prepared to book the car well in advance (ask at your hotel), and be especially alert when driving in the city. Roads are often very wide and lanes are not clearly marked. The speed limit is 60 kph (37 mph) in town, 90 kph (56 mph) elsewhere. It is advisable to stick to these limits, not least because road surfaces can suddenly deteriorate. Main country roads are generally dual-carriageway with no central reservation, but motorways are few and those that exist do not conform to Western standards.

Drive on the right, and do not cross a central single or double unbroken line. Priority is to the right, and trams and buses come before cars, so give them a wide birth. Seat belts are compulsory for drivers and front seat passengers. Road signs are international, and parking is generally not too much of a problem in the Soviet Union. Drinking and driving is not permitted.

If you are involved in an accident, contact your nearest Intourist Office (**бюрó Интурúста**/*byooro Intoorista*) immediately.

| | |
|---|---|
| **Мне нýжна машúна** <br> *Mnye nuzhna mashina* | I need a car |
| **Мне нýжно заказáть машúну** <br> *Mnye nuzhna zakazat mashinoo* | I need to order a car |
| **Где я могý остáвить машúну?** <br> *Gdye ya magoo astavit mashinoo?* | Where can I park? |

Petrol comes in litres:

**три́дцать ли́тров, пожа́луйста**    *tridtsat litraf, pazhalasta*    30 litres please

You will find these words connected with motoring useful:

| | | | |
|---|---|---|---|
| **доро́га** *daroga* | road | **води́тельские права́** *vadityelskiye prava* | driving licence |
| **маршру́т** *marshroot* | route | **перекрёсток** *pirikrostok* | cross roads |
| **шоссе́** *shassay* | main road | **запра́вочная кало́нка** *zapravachnaya kalonka* | service station |
| **автодоро́га** *aftodaroga* | motorway | **ма́сло и вода́** *maslo i vada* | oil and water |
| **светофо́р** *svyetafor* | traffic lights | **мнлиционе́р** *militsianer* | policeman |

For a list of car parts, see p. 114.

## *Road signs*

| | |
|---|---|
| ДЕРЖИТЕСЬ ПРАВОЙ СТОРОНЫ | Keep to the right |
| ВЪЕЗД ЗАПРЕЩЕН | No entry |
| СТОЯНКА ЗАПРЕЩЕНА | No stopping |
| ОДНОСТОРОННЕЕ ДВИЖЕНИЕ | One-way traffic |
| ОБЪЕЗД | Detour |
| ОПАСНО | Danger |

# *the way it works*

## *Taking the tube*

The verb to use when you're going by some form of transport is
**е́хать**/*yekhat* (to go):

| | |
|---|---|
| **я е́ду**/*ya yedoo* | I go |
| **ты е́дешь**/*ty yedish* | you go |
| **он/она́ е́дет**/*on/ana yedit* | he/she goes |
| **мы е́дем**/*my yedim* | we go |
| **вы е́дете**/*vy yeditye* | you go |
| **они́ е́дут**/*ani yedoot* | they go |
| Я е́ду на по́езде | I go by train |
| на маши́не | by car |
| на такси́ | by taxi |
| Алис е́дет на метро́ | Alice goes by Metro |
| на трамва́е | by tram |
| на тролле́йбусе | by trolleybus |

Note however that if it's the actual train, car etc. you're talking about, then
you use **идти́**: По́езд **идёт** бы́стро/*Poyizd idyot bystra* (The train is going
fast).

*Talking about possessions (the genitive case)*

(*a*)  The group's luggage; the luggage of the group: When we say ''s' or 'of the' in English, in Russian there is a special case – the possessive or genitive case. Masculine and neuter nouns take an **-a** (those ending in **й**, a soft sign or **e** take **я**) and feminine nouns lose their ending in **-a** and take **-ы** (or **-и** for those ending in **-я**, a soft sign, or after **г, к, х, ж, ч, ш** and **щ**).

| | |
|---|---|
| Vadim's trip | **Поéздка Вáдима**/*Payezdka Vadima* |
| Lena's watch | **Часы́ Лéны**/*Chasy Lyeny* |

Adjectives in the genitive case drop their normal endings and take **-ого/-его** (*-ovo/-yevo*) with masculine and neuter nouns, **-ой/-ей** (*-oi/-yei*) with feminine nouns. Again, you will hear all these different endings, but don't worry too much about getting them right yourself.

(*b*)  The genitive case is used after certain prepositions. Here are some of them: **для**/*dlya* (for); **до**/*do* (to, up, to, as far as, before); **из**/*iz* (from, out of); **от**/*ot* (from); **без**/*byez* (without) – also used when telling the time (see p. 35).

| | |
|---|---|
| Я éду до стáнции ''Университéт'' | I'm going to 'University' station |
| Этот пóезд прихóдит из Москвы́ | This train comes from Moscow |

Pronouns in the genitive are the same as in the accusative case: **меня́, тебя́, егó** (**негó** after a preposition), **её** (**неё** after a preposition), **нас, вас, их** (**них** after a preposition):

| | |
|---|---|
| Это для меня́? – Да, э́то для вас | Is it for me? – Yes, it's for you |

*things to do*

.1  **Pronunciation practice**   It's important to be able to read the names of stations when travelling on the Metro; here are some of the places you may want to go to:

### КИ́ЕВСКАЯ   АРБА́ТСКАЯ   КРОПО́ТКИНСКАЯ
### БИБЛИОТЕ́КА   И́МЕНИ ЛЕ́НИНА   ПЛО́ЩАДЬ СВЕРДЛО́ВА

Here are three more signs you will see when travelling by Metro. What do you think they mean?

### ОЛУСТИ́ТЕ* 5 КОПЕ́ЕК   К ПОЕЗДА́М   ВЫ́ХОД В ГО́РОД

* **опусти́ть**/*apoostit* to lower

**4.2**  You are peering at a Russian map and trying to work out where everything is. See if you can match the items below with the appropriate signs:

(a)  остано́вка авто́буса
(b)  запра́вочная коло́нка
(c)  ста́нция метро́
(d)  светофо́р
(e)  стоя́нка такси́

**4**

**1**

**2**

**3**

**5**

**4.3**  Now you should be able to make yourself understood on all forms of transport. Here's the test!

1  You need to get back to your hotel, but can't see the Metro station. What do you ask a passerby?

2  You're on the Metro and looking for the station Prospekt Mira. Can you ask a fellow traveller where it is on the map?

3  You decide to take a trolleybus. Can you ask a passer-by where the stop is?

4  You're in a taxi. Ask the driver to take you to the theatre.

5  You're at a service station and need some petrol (**бензи́н**/benzeen). Ask for 40 litres.

## MUSEUMS AND ENTERTAINMENT

▶▶ **Out and about in Moscow**   Whether you are on a tour, or have time off during a business trip, a visit to the **Kremlin** (**Кремль**/*Kreml*) – Moscow's ancient walled citadel – is a must. From **Red Square**, where the fairy-tale cathedral of St Basil (**храм Васи́лия Блаже́нного**/*khram Vasiliya Blazhennava*) attracts visitors worldwide, the main entrance, for official visitors only, is the gate by the famous Spassky clock tower (**Спа́сская ба́шня**/*Spasskaya bashnya*) – one of 20 such towers along the Kremlin walls. The public entrance to the Kremlin is the Trinity Gate. Once inside, you will see the Belfry of Ivan the Great, the tallest of the Kremlin buildings, with the enormous Tsar's Bell (**Царь колоко́л**/*Tsar kolakol*) at its foot. There are several splendid gold-domed churches inside the Kremlin walls, among them the Assumption Cathedral (**Успе́нский собо́р**/*Usspenskiy sabor*) where coronations once took place, the Annunciation Cathedral (**Благове́щенский собо́р**/ *Blagaveshchenskiy sabor*) where the tsars attended services and the Cathedral of the Archangel Michael (**Арха́нгельский собо́р**/*Arkhangilskiy sabor*) where you can see many of their tombs, including that of Ivan the Terrible. These cathedrals are open to the public, but tickets must be bought first from the cash desk in the Trinity Gardens.

Anyone can stroll around the Kremlin complex between dawn and dusk, but not all of the buildings are open to the public. Of those that are, however, the most fascinating for its contents is without doubt the Armoury (**Оружейная палата**/*Oruzheinaya palata*). Now a museum, it contains amongst other things the coaches, jewels, crowns and thrones of the tsars, and the magnificent costumes of Catherine the Great.

▶ ▶ ▶ **Museum opening times** vary considerably, so it is worth checking up first, but most open around 10 am and close at 6 or 7 pm. Many museums shut on Mondays (some on Tuesdays) as well as the first or last day of the month for cleaning, but are open all day Sunday. Museums are closed on public holidays. There is usually a small entrance charge, and you will have to leave coats, bags and cameras in the cloakroom.

## в музее/at the museum

It is late afternoon, and Donald decides he's just got time to visit another museum before returning to the hotel. He finds his way successfully, but he's not sure what time the museum closes, so he asks at the ticket window (**касса**).

| | |
|---|---|
| Donald: | **Простите, в котором часу закрывается музей?** *Prastitye, v katoram chasoo zakryvaitsa muzei?* |
| Cashier: | **В восемь часов.** *V vosyem chasof.* |
| Donald: | **Отлично. Один билет, пожалуйста – и дайте мне каталог.** *Atlichna. Adin bilyet, pazhalasta, i daitye mnye katalok.* |
| Cashier: | **Извините, здесь нельзя фотографировать. Надо оставить аппарат в гардеробе.** *Izvinitye, zdyes nilzya fatagrafiravat. Nada astavit apparat v gardirobye.* |

гардероб

**простите** excuse me      **отлично** excellent

*Visiting a museum or gallery*

**Когда открывается галерея?**     When does the gallery open?
*Kugda atkryvayitsa galereya?*
**В котором часу закрывается музей?**     What time does the museum close?
*V katoram chasoo zakryvayitsa muzei?*

**Оди́н биле́т, пожа́луйста**
*Adin bilyet, pazhalasta*

One ticket please

**Да́йте мне/ско́лько сто́ит катало́г?**
*Daitye mnye/skolka stoit katalok?*

Give me/how much is a catalogue?

**На́до оста́вить аппара́т в гардеро́бе**
*Nada astavit apparat v garderobye*

You have to leave your camera in
the cloakroom

▶▶▶ **Planning an outing**   Most Russians book tickets for theatres, concerts
etc. well ahead, and tickets for the really popular venues such as the
Bolshoi Theatre (**Большо́й теа́тр**), the Conservatoire of Music
(**Консервато́рия**/*Conservatoriya*), the modern theatres Sovrimyenik
(**Совреме́нник**) and Taganka (**Теа́тр на Тага́нке**/*Tiatr na Taganki*)
are hard to come by if you have not pre-booked. Your hotel service
bureau may be able to obtain tickets for you, or you can try through
Intourist. Failing that you can go to the theatre itself and see if you
can get a return on the night.

▶▶▶ **Theatre and concert performances** usually start at 7.00 or 7.30 pm
(there may be a Sunday matinee at 12.00). After the usherette has
torn off the **контро́ль**/*kantrol* part of your ticket, deposit your coat,
umbrella etc. in the cloakroom (**гардеро́б**/*garderob*) and pick up a
cloakroom ticket (**номеро́к**/*namirok*). You'll probably be asked if
you want to hire binoculars (**бино́кль ну́жен?**/*binokl nuzhen?*) for a
small fee – if you do, this gives you the advantage of jumping the
cloakroom queue when returning them at the end of the
performance (**спекта́кль**/*spiktakl*). You'll probably want a
programme (**програ́мма**) and if you're not sure where you're
sitting, ask: **Где моё ме́сто?**/*Gdye mayo myesta?*

## что вам хочется посмотреть?/what would you like to see?

Lucy decides she would like to go to the ballet or to a concert if she can manage to get a ticket. She discusses it with Vadim.

Lucy: **Я о́чень хочу́ пойти́ на бале́т и́ли на конце́рт сего́дня ве́чером, и́ли мо́жет быть посмотре́ть ру́сский фильм.**
*Ya ochin khachoo paeetee na balyet ili na kantsert sivodnya vyecheram, ili mozhet byt pasmatryet rooskiy film.*

(Vadim picks up 'Leisure in Moscow' and scans the pages)

Vadim: **Посмо́трим ... В Ма́лом теа́тре идёт ''Дя́дя Ва́ня'', пье́са Че́хова, в Большо́м теа́тре даю́т бале́т ''Жизе́ль'', и во Дворце́ съе́здов игра́ет Моско́вский Госуда́рственный Орке́стр. Вы лю́бите му́зыку?**
*Pasmotrim ... V Malam tiatri idyot 'Dyadya Vanya', pyesa Chekhava, v Balshom tiatri dayoot balyet 'Zhizel', i va Dvartse syezdaf igrayet Maskovskiy Gasudarstvinniy Arkestr. Vy lyoobitye muzykoo?*

Lucy: **Да, о́чень люблю́!**
*Da, ochin lublyoo!*

| | | | |
|---|---|---|---|
| **мо́жет быть** | perhaps | **Посмо́трим** | Let's see |
| **пье́са Че́хова** | a play by Chekhov | **му́зыка** | music |

### Что идёт сегодня вечером в театре? *What's on at the theatre this evening?*

| | |
|---|---|
| **Я о́чень хочу́ пойти́ ...** | I'd love to go ... |
| *Ya ochin khachoo paeetee ...* | |
| **в теа́тр/в кино́/на бале́т** | to the theatre/cinema/ballet |
| *v tiatr/v kino/na balyet* | |
| **в о́перу/на конце́рт** | to the opera/a concert |
| *v opiroo/na kantsert* | |
| **посмотре́ть фильм/пье́су** | to see a film/play |
| *pasmatryet film/pyesoo* | |

**"Дя́дя Ва́ня" идёт в Ма́лом теа́тре**
*Dyadya Vanya idyot v Malam tiatri*
**Даю́т бале́т "Жизе́ль" в Большо́м теа́тре**
*Dayoot balyet Zhizel v Balshom tiatri*

Uncle Vanya is on at the Maly Theatre
They're doing the ballet Giselle at the Bolshoi Theatre

**Моско́вский Госуда́рственный Орке́стр игра́ет ...**
*Maskovskiy Gasudarstvyenniy Arkestr igrayet ...*

The Moscow State Orchestra is playing ...

**... в Кремлёвском Дворце́ съе́здов**
*... v Krimlyovskam Dvartse syedzdaf*

... at the Kremlin Palace of Congresses

## в театра́льной ка́ссе/at the theatre box office

Lucy tries her luck at the Bolshoi Theatre, so she and Donald rush off to see if they can get tickets:

Lucy:  **Два биле́та на сего́дня**, пожа́луйста, **на "Жизе́ль".**
*Dva bilyeta na sivodnya, pazhalasta, na 'Zhizel'.*

Cashier:  **На сего́дня все биле́ты про́даны. У меня́ оста́лось то́лько три-четы́ре ме́ста на за́втра.**
*Na sivodnya vsye bilyety prodany. U minya astalas tolka tri-chetirye myesta na zaftra.*

**все биле́ты про́даны**  all the tickets are sold

Disappointed, they go to the concert hall to see if they can get seats. They queue by a sign saying **"Прода́жа биле́тов на сего́дня"** (*Tickets for today's performance*).

Lucy:  **У вас есть биле́ты на сего́дняшний концéрт?**
*U vas yest bilyety na sivodnyashniy kantsert?*

Cashier:  **Да. Вы хоти́те балко́н или амфитеа́тр?**
*Da. Vy khatitye balkon ili amfitiatr?*

Lucy:  **Два ме́ста на балко́не**, пожа́луйста.
*Dva myesta na balkone, pazhalasta.*

Cashier:  **Вот они́ – пя́тый ряд, пра́вая сторона́.**
*Vot ani – pyatiy ryad, pravaya starana.*

Lucy:  **Скажи́те, когда́ начина́ется концéрт?**
*Skazhitye, kugda nachinaitsa kantsert?*

Cashier:  **В семь часо́в, че́рез два́дцать мину́т. Вы пришли́ как раз во́время!**
*V syem chasof, chiryez dvatsat minoot. Vy prishli kak raz vovremya!*

**ряд, сторона́**  row, side     **че́рез два́дцать мину́т**  in 20 minutes
**Вы пришли́ как раз во́время!**  You have come just in time!

## Buying a ticket

**Два билета на сегодня/на завтра/на вторник**
*Dva bilyeta na sivodnya/na zaftra/na ftornik*
2 tickets for today/tomorrow/Tuesday

**Два места на "Жизель"/на "Русалку"**
*Dva myesta na Zhizel/na Rusalkoo*
2 seats for 'Giselle'/for 'Rusalka'

**У вас есть билеты на сегодняшний концерт?**
*U vas yest bilyety na sivodnyashniy kantsert?*
Do you have any tickets for today's concert?

**Все билеты проданы**
*Vsye bilyety prodany*
All the tickets are sold

**У меня осталось только три-четыре места на завтра**
*U minya astalas tolka tri-chetirye myesta na zaftra*
I've got only 3 or 4 seats for tomorrow

**на второе июня/на первое февраля**
*na ftaroye iyoonya/na pyervaye fivralya*
for 2nd June/for 1st February

**Вы хотите балкон или амфитеатр?**
*Vy khatitye balkon ili amfitiatr?*
Do you want balcony or amphitheatre?

**на балконе, на бельэтаже**
*na balkoni, byeletazhé*
in the balcony, dress circle

**. . . в партере**
*. . . v parteri*
. . . in the stalls

**ряд пятый, правая/левая сторона**
*ryad pyatiy, pravaya/lyevaya starana*
row 5, right/left hand side

**Когда начинается концерт/представление?**
*Kugda nachinaitsa kantsert/pridstavlyeniye?*
When does the concert/performance begin?

**Начало в 19 часов, цена 3 рубля пятьдесят коп.**
*Nachala v 19 chasof, tsena 3 rooblya 50 kop.*
It starts at 7 pm, price 3r. 50k.

Look on your ticket and you'll see which part of the auditorium you're sitting in:

| | |
|---|---|
| **ложа** | a box |
| **оркестр** | orchestra pit |
| **партер** | stalls |
| **амфитеатр** | amphitheatre |
| **балкон** | balcony |
| **бельэтаж** | dress circle |
| **первый ярус** | first circle |
| **второй ярус** | second circle |
| **галерея** | gallery |

You will also see the date, the time the performance starts, your row and seat number and whether it's on the right, left or in the middle (**середина**/*siridina*). For dates, see p. 113.

If your Russian is not up to a play or a film, you can always go to the circus (**цирк**/*tsirk*), or to a musical at the Stanislavsky and Nemirovich-Danchenko Musical Theatre, to an operetta at the Operetta Theatre (**Моско́вский теа́тр опере́тты**/*Maskovskiy tiatr opirety*) or to a show at the Puppet Theatre (**Центра́льный теа́тр ку́кол**/*Tsintralniy tiatr kukal*).

## the way it works

### Reflexive verbs

You may have noticed that some verbs end in **ся** or **сь**. These are called reflexive verbs (the verb reflects the action of the speaker, and the ending **ся** can often be translated by 'self'). Many verbs can be either reflexive or non-reflexive, e.g. **открыва́ть** to open, **открыва́ться** to be open (lit. open itself).

Reflexive verbs ending in **-аться** take these endings:

| | |
|---|---|
| -а́юсь | -а́емся |
| -а́ешься | -а́етесь |
| -а́ется | -а́ются |

## В Большом театре *At the Bolshoi . . .*

**Большой** (*balshoi*) and **малый** (*maly*) are adjectives meaning 'large' and 'small' (though the more usual adjective for small is **маленький**/*malinkiy*). Adjectives in the locative case (i.e. after **в** or **на** when there is no movement involved) end in

| | |
|---|---|
| **-ом/-ем** for masculine and neuter nouns: | в Малом театре<br>(at the Little Theatre) |
| **-ой/-ей** for feminine nouns: | на Красной площади<br>(in Red Square) |

## Весь/*vyes All*

This is an adjective, and occurs in all sorts of useful expressions:

| | | |
|---|---|---|
| **весь день** (masc.) | *vyes dyen* | all day |
| **всю неделю\*** (fem.) | *vsyoo nidyelyoo* | all week |
| **всё время** (neuter) | *vsyo vryemya* | all the time |
| **все люди** (plural) | *vsye lyoodi* | all people |

**всё** on its own in the neuter form means 'all', 'everything' (and sometimes 'all the time').

\*Expressions of time are often in the accusative case – the nominative case in the feminine is **вся**/*vsya* (**неделя**/*nidyelya* = week).

### *Expressions of time*

| | | |
|---|---|---|
| **вчера** | *fchera* | yesterday |
| **сегодня утром** | *sivodnya utram* | this morning |
| **сегодня вечером** | *sivodnya vyecheram* | this evening |
| **завтра ночью** | *zaftra nochyoo* | tomorrow night |
| **на прошлой неделе** | *na proshloi nidyeli* | last week |
| **на будущей неделе** | *na boodooshchei nidyeli* | next week |

## *things to do*

**4.4**    **Pronunciation practice**    You'll probably see these signs in the theatre or cinema. Pronounce them correctly, and say what you think they mean:

НЕЛЬЗЯ КУРИТЬ В КИНО

АДМИНИСТРАТОР

КУРИТЕЛЬНАЯ КОМНАТА

ФОЙЕ

**4.5**

---

### Центральный Музей Исскувста

Музей открыт с 9.$^{00}$ до 20.$^{00}$, касса работает до 19.$^{30}$ ч.
Выходный день: понедельник
Санитарный день: последний день каждого месяца

---

1 If you wanted to visit this museum on a Tuesday, would you be able to get in?
2 You have an hour to spare before meeting a friend at 8 o'clock. Would it be a good idea to go to the museum?
3 Apart from the last day of the month, at what other times is the museum closed?

**4.6**

1 For what date is this ticket valid?
2 In what part of the theatre would you be sitting, and on what side?
3 What row and seat number?

---

### БОЛЬШОЙ ТЕАТР

Б/кн. No. четверг 13 июня 1989 года

000735  вечер  БЕЛЬЭТАЖ  левая сторона

ряд 8        место 5

цена 2 р. 30 к.

---

**4.7** You are the only person in your group who speaks Russian, and have been persuaded to make enquiries at the booking office on behalf of your friends. How would you cope with their requests?

1 Ian and Hilary want two tickets in the balcony for tomorrow.
2 Judy wants to know what time the performance starts.
3 Elizabeth wants a ticket in the stalls – in the middle – for this evening.
4 James and Sarah want to know if there are any seats for today's concert.
5 The cashier only has tickets for 7 February. What does she say?

## CHANGING MONEY

By far the easiest way to change money (**де́ньги**/*dyengi*) is simply to go to your hotel currency exchange desk (**обме́н де́нег**/*abmyen dyenek*). You will need the currency declaration you filled out at customs, and you will be given a receipt (**квита́нция**/*kvitantsiya*) for the transaction. You can also change money at airports and banks (banking hours are approximately 9.30 am to 12.30 pm from Monday to Friday). Traveller's cheques and foreign currency can be used in Intourist hotels and restaurants and in the hard currency shops reserved for foreigners.

The Russian **rouble** (**рубль**/*roobl*, pl. **рубли́**/*roobli*), is divided into 100 **kopecks** (**копе́йка**/*kapyeika*, pl. **копе́йки**/*kapyeiki*). Roubles come in notes of up to 100 r., and there is a silver-coloured 1-rouble coin. Kopecks are either silver or copper coins.

### мне надо обменять деньги/I need to change some money

Mike Nash and his group of students plan to spend the day shopping, but Mike realises he is running short of money. He goes to the hotel exchange bureau.

Mike: **Здесь мо́жно разменя́ть доро́жные че́ки?**
*Zdyes mozhna razminyat darozhniye cheky?*

Clerk: **Да, мо́жно.**
*Da, mozhna.*

Mike: **Я та́кже хочу́ обменя́ть англи́йскую валю́ту – де́сять фу́нтов.**
*Ya takzhe khachoo abminyat angliskuyoo valyootoo – dyesyat foontaf.*

Clerk: **Да́йте ваш па́спорт, пожа́луйста, и ва́шу\* деклара́цию.**
*Daitye vash paspart, pazhalasta, i vashoo diklaratsiyoo.*

(Mike hands over the documents)

**Тепе́рь распиши́тесь ... Пожалуйста, вот вам тридцать рубле́й, и квита́нция.**
*Tipyer raspishityes ... Pazhalasta, vot vam tridsat rooblei i kvitantsiya.*

Mike: **А па́спорт где?**
*A paspart gdye?*

Clerk: **О прости́те ми́стер Наш – вот он.**
*O prastitye mister Nash – vot on.*

\* **ва́шу** is the accusative form of **ва́ша**.

*Changing money*

| | |
|---|---|
| **Где ближа́йший банк/Го́сбанк/обме́н де́нег?** *Gdye blizhaishiy bank/Gosbank/abmyen dyenek?* | Where's the nearest bank/ State bank/currency exchange? |
| **Мо́жно разменя́ть доро́жные че́ки?** *Mozhna razminyat darozhnye cheki?* | Can I change traveller's cheques? |
| **... обменя́ть англи́йскую валю́ту?** *... abminyat angliskuyoo valyootoo?* | ... change some English currency? |
| **... америка́нские до́ллары/англи́йские фу́нты** *... amerikanskiye dollary/angliskiye foonty* | ... American dollars/ English pounds |
| **Како́й сего́дня ку́рс?** *Kakoi sivodnya koors?* | What's the exchange rate today? |
| **Ско́лько вам ну́жно?** *Skolka vam nuzhna?* | How much do you need? |
| **де́сять фу́нтов/два́дцать до́лларов** *dyesyat foontaf/dvatsat dollaraf* | ten pounds/twenty dollars |
| **Распиши́тесь – вот 30 рубле́й, и квита́нция** *Raspishityes – vot 30 rooblyei, i kvitantsiya* | Sign here – here's 30 roubles and your receipt |

64

## *the way it works*

### *Recognising the genitive plural; numbers and money*

You have probably noticed the ending **-ов** (sometimes **-ев**) in expressions such as **шесть часо́в** (six o'clock). This is one of the genitive plural endings in Russian. The genitive plural is always used after numbers from five upwards. This is how many nouns behave in the genitive plural:

| *masculine* | *neuter* | *feminine* |
|---|---|---|
| **пять фу́нтов** | **де́сять мест** | **во́семь газе́т** |
| *pyat foontaf* | *dyesyat myest* | *vosyem gazyet* |
| five pounds | ten places | eight papers |
| (adds **-ов**) | (drops the **-о**) | (drops the **-a**) |

Nouns ending in **e** or a soft sign take **-ей** in the genitive plural:

**два́дцать площаде́й**   *dvatsat plashchadyei*   twenty squares

The number 1 takes the nominative singular, but numbers 2, 3, and 4 are followed by the genitive singular in Russian. This is how it works for money:

| | | | |
|---|---|---|---|
| **оди́н рубль** | 1 rouble | **одна́ копе́йка** | 1 kopeck |
| *adin roobl* | | *adna kapyeika* | |
| **три рубля́** | 3 roubles | **три копе́йки** | 3 kopecks |
| *tree rooblya* | | *tree kapyeiki* | |
| **шесть рубле́й** | 6 roubles | **шесть копе́ек** | 6 kopecks |
| *shest rooblyei* | | *shest kapayek* | |

It's complicated, but don't worry! For money you'll soon recognise these expressions, and generally speaking you can avoid using different endings for numbers by saying or pointing to what you want, then giving the number, e.g.

**Бу́лочка – пять, пожа́луйста**   Roll – 5 please
*Boolachka, pyat pazhalasta*
**Моро́женое – три, пожа́луйста**   Ice cream – 3 please
*Marozhenaye, tree pazhalasta*

## things to do

**5.1**   You are running short of cash, so you go along to the currency exchange bureau in your hotel.

  1   Ask if you can change some American dollars.
  2   Ask if you can change £25.
  3   See if it's possible to change traveller's cheques.
  4   Ask what the exchange rate is today.

**5.2**   You go into a bank to change money, and the clerk says to you: **Дайте вашу деклара́цию, пожа́луйста**. Does he want

  (*a*)   your receipt
  (*b*)   your currency declaration form
  (*c*)   your traveller's cheques?

**5.3**   You go over to the cash desk with your chit, and the cashier says: **Вот вам со́рок пять рубле́й два́дцать копе́ек**. Is he giving you:

  (*a*)   25 r. 12 kop.      (*b*)   40 r. 25 kop.      (*c*)   45 r. 20 kop. ?

**5.4**   Ask for the following items in Russian, without using the genitive plural:

  2 ice creams      4 fruit juices      6 tickets      10 postcards

## SHOPPING FOR FOOD

If you want to buy food, go to a **гастроно́м**/*gastranom*, a large foodstore with different departments (or in a smaller place look for **проду́кты**/*pradukty* or **про́дмаг**/*prodmag*). Many individual food shops in the Soviet Union simply have signs bearing the name of the product, so for a butcher's you would see **мя́со**/*myasa* (meat), a fishmonger's **ры́ба**/*ryba* (fish), a baker's **хлеб**/*khlep* (bread), a dairy **молоко́**/*malako* (milk), and so on. However, you will also see these names of common food shops:

| | |
|---|---|
| **бу́лочная**/*boolachnaya* | baker's |
| **конди́терская**/*kandityerskaya* | cakeshop |
| **моло́чная**/*malochnaya* | dairy |
| **о́вощи-фру́кты**/*ovashchi-frookty* | greengrocer's |
| **бакале́я**/*bakaleya* | grocer's |
| **мя́со-пти́ца**/*myasa-ptitsa* | meat and poultry |

As well as at the greengrocer's, Russians like to buy their fruit and vegetables at the market (**ры́нок**/*rynak*) where prices may be high but there is much more variety. Markets are always very busy at weekends and the day before a public holiday, and it's best to go early in the morning. There are sometimes shortages of basic foods in the shops, and fruit and vegetables are generally restricted to what is in season. Though some food shops are now self-service (look out for the sign **универса́м**/*universam*, supermarket), in many you still have to queue at the counter and then at the cash desk where you'll need to obtain a receipt (**чек**/*chek*) before you can collect your goods.

## в гастрономе/in the foodstore

Alice and Sergei are feeling rather hungry, and take a look round a foodstore. They decide to buy some fruit and some bread.

Sergei: **Ско́лько сто́ят я́блоки?**
*Skolka stoyat yablaki?*

Assistant: Два рубля́ кило́.
*Dva rooblya kilo.*

Sergei: **Я возьму́ кило́**, пожа́луйста, и пятьсо́т грамм помидо́ров.
*Ya vazmoo kilo, pazhalasta, i pyatsot gram pamidoraf.*

Alice: Ой Серге́й, ви́дишь краси́вый виногра́д – да́йте нам и виногра́д то́же.
*Oi, Sergei, vidish krasiviy vinagrad – daitye nam i vinagrad tozhe.*

(They move on to the bread counter.)

Alice: **Да́йте мне** чёрный хлеб, пожа́луйста, и две* бу́лочки.
*Daitye mnye chorniy khlep, pazhalasta, i dvye boolachki.*

Assistant: Ещё чтó-нибудь?
*Yisho shto-niboot?*

Sergei: Да, вон то пиро́жное и э́ту коро́бку конфе́т.
*Da, von to pirozhnaye i etoo karopkoo kanfyet.*

Alice: Кака́я жа́дность! У вас по кра́йней ме́ре де́ньги есть?
*Kakaya zhadnast! U vas po krainyei myeri dyengi yest?*

Sergei: Ка́жется у меня́ совсе́м нет ме́лочи …
*Kazhitsa u minya savsyem nyet myelachi …*

| | |
|---|---|
| ви́дишь краси́вый виногра́д | look at those lovely grapes |
| кака́я жа́дность! | what greed! |
| по кра́йней ме́ре | at least |
| Ка́жется у меня́ совсе́м нет ме́лочи … | I don't seem to have any change at all … |

*Remember that you use **две** for 'two' with feminine nouns.

## Buying something to eat

Don't forget that the metric system of weights and measures operates in the Soviet Union:

**Яблоки стоят два рубля кило**
*Yablaki stoyat dva rooblya kilo*
**Дайте нам сто грамм/полкило**
*Daitye nam sto gram/polkilo*
**... пятьсот грамм помидоров/кило яблок**
*... pyatsot gram pamidoraf/kilo yablak*

The apples cost 2 roubles a kilo
Give us 100 grams, half a kilo
... 500 grams of tomatoes/ a kilo of apples

To avoid using the genitive case endings, once again you can simply say:

| | | |
|---|---|---|
| **огурцы – пятьсот грамм** | *agurtsy – pyatsot gram* | cucumbers – 500 g. |
| **персики – кило** | *persiki – kilo* | peaches – a kilo |
| **яблоки – два кило** | *yablaki – dva kilo* | apples – 2 kilos |

**Bread**  If you go into a **булочная** or a **булочная-кондитерская**, you will find all kinds of different bread and rolls on sale. A **буханка**/*bukhanka* is a long loaf, usually brown, and a **батон**/*baton* is a large round white loaf. Russians are very fond of rye bread (**ржаной хлеб**/*rzhanoi khlep*). You can also buy cake (**кекс**/*keks*), sweets (**конфеты**/*konfyety*) and chocolate (**шоколад**/*shakalat*).

**Дайте мне чёрную буханку и две булочки**
*Daitye mnye chornuyoo bukhankoo i dvye boolachki*
**... вон то пирожное и ту коробку конфет**
*... von to pirozhnaye i too karopkoo kanfyet*

Give me a brown loaf and 2 rolls
... that pastry and that box of sweets

Use these expressions when buying food:

| | |
|---|---|
| a bunch of grapes | **кисть винограда**/*kist vinagrada* |
| a jar of pickles | **банка солёных**/*banka salyonykh* |
| a tin of sardines | **коробка сардин**/*karopka sardin* |
| a box of sweets | **коробка конфет**/*karopka kanfyet* |
| a bar of chocolate | **плитка шоколада**/*plitka shakalada* |

 For a list of groceries, see p. 114.

# MAKING PURCHASES 2

At the **БЕРЁЗКА** (Beriozka) shops and other hard currency stores, you can buy souvenirs, food, duty-free drink and many other goods for pounds or dollars (though prices may be quoted in roubles). You will also be able to use your credit card (**кредитная карточка**/*kreditnaya kartachka*) for goods bought here and in Intourist hotels. There is often a better choice than you will find outside, but nonetheless you will probably want to look round a typical Russian department store (**универмаг**/*univermag*), such as **ГУМ**/*GUM* – an abbreviation for **Государственный Универсальный Магазин** (State Universal Store) – in Moscow, or **ЦУМ**/*TSUM* – **Центральный Универсальный Магазин** (Central Universal Store) – in Leningrad. Look out for these shops or departments: **меха**/*mixha* (furs), **часы**/*chasy* (watches and clocks), **грампластинки**/*gramplastinki* (records), and **игрушки**/*igrushki* (toys). Department stores are usually crowded, so be ready to use your elbows, and persevere! Opening times vary from shop to shop, but most are open from 9.00 am to 7.00 or 8.00 pm from Monday to Saturday (except on public holidays). Food shops may open earlier and close for lunch between 1.00 and 2.00 pm. Here are the names of some common shops:

| | |
|---|---|
| bookshop | **книжный магазин**/*knizhniy magazin* |
| chemist's | **аптека**/*aptyeka* |
| electrical goods | **электротовары**/*elektratavary* |
| hardware | **скобяной магазин**/*skabyanoi magazin* |
| jeweller's | **ювелирный магазин**/*yoovilirniy magazin* |
| music, games, sport etc. | **культтовары**/*kulttavary* (lit. culture goods) |
| photographic supplies | **фототовары**/*fotatavary* |
| second-hand shop | **комиссионный магазин**/*kamissioniy magazin* |
| stationer's | **канцтовары**/*kantstavary* |

The names of many shops begin with **дом**/*dom* … (which means 'house'), e.g. **Дом игру́шки**/*Dom igrushki* (House of the toy), **Дом кни́ги**/*Dom knigi* (House of the book), **Дом о́буви**/*Dom oboovi* (House of footwear, i.e. shoe shop).

▶ ▶ ▶ **Souvenirs** When shopping for things to take home, you will find a variety of goods made from amber (**янта́рь**/*yantar*), silver (**серебро́**/*siribro*) and glass (**стекло́**/*stiklo*). Little gifts might include a headscarf (**плато́к**/*platok*), shawl (**шаль**/*shal*), tablecloth (**ска́терть**/*skatirt*), painted wooden spoon (**ло́жка**/*lozhka*) or tray (**подно́с**/*padnos*). You might also want to buy a nest of dolls (**матрёшка**/*matrioshka*) or a fur cap with earflaps (**уша́нка**/*ushanka*). Here are some more typically Russian items:

| | |
|---|---|
| abacus | **счёт**/*sshot* |
| amber brooch | **янта́рная бро́шка**/*yantarnaya broshka* |
| amber necklace, earrings | **янта́рные бу́сы, се́рьги**/*yantarnye boosy, sergi* |
| camera | **фотоаппара́т**/*fotaapparat* |
| ceramics | **кера́мика**/*keramika* |
| enamel | **эма́ль**/*emal* |
| icon | **ико́на**/*ikona* |
| lace | **кру́жево**/*kruzheva* |
| leather | **ко́жа**/*kozha* |

## купить сувениры/buying souvenirs

Alice is looking for presents to take home, and heads for the **ПОДАРКИ**/*Padarki* (Gifts) department in a large store. She has seen a little samovar in the window, and wants to know how much it costs.

Alice: **Покажи́те**, пожа́луйста, ма́ленький самова́р **в витри́не**.
*Pakazhitye, pazhalasta, malinkiy samavar v vitrinye.*
Assistant: (pointing) **Э́тот?**
*Etat?*
Alice: **Не э́тот, а тот, ря́дом** – чёрный с цвета́ми. **Да, э́тот!**
**Ско́лько он сто́ит?**
*Ni etat, a tot, ryadam – chorny s tsvitami. Da, etat! Skolka on stoit?*
Assistant: **Сто́ит со́рок пять рубле́й.**
*Stoit sorak pyat rooblyei.*
Alice: **Бо́же мой, э́то сли́шком до́рого!** Лу́чше что́-нибудь
подеше́вле …
*Bozhe moi, eta slishkam dorakga! Loochshe shto-niboot podishevli …*

**Бо́же мой!** My god!

## How to buy something 2

In many shops and stores in the Soviet Union, there are three distinct steps to making purchases:

**1 Choosing** Ask the assistant to show you what you want:

| | |
|---|---|
| **Покажи́те пожа́луйста ма́ленький самова́р в витри́не** <br> *Pokazhitye pazhalasta malinkiy samavar v vitrinye* | Can you show me the little samovar in the window |
| **Не э́тот, а тот, ря́дом** <br> *Ni etat, a tot, ryadam* | Not this one – that one, next to it |
| **чёрный с цвета́ми** <br> *chorny s tsvitami* | the black one with flowers |
| **Нет, не на́до – э́то сли́шком до́рого** <br> *Nyet, ni nada – eta slishkam dorakga* | No, I don't want it – it's too expensive |
| **Лу́чше что́-нибудь подеше́вле** <br> *Loochshe shto-niboot podishevli* | I'd rather have (lit. better) something cheaper |
| **Вы́пишите чек, я его́/её возьму́** <br> *Vypishitye chek, ya yevo/yeyo vazmoo* | Write out a chit, I'll take it |
| **Плати́те в ка́ссу со́рок пять рубле́й** <br> *Platitye v kassoo sorak pyat rooblyei* | Pay at the cash desk, 45 r. |

**2 Paying** Take your chit (**чек**/*chek*) and go to the cash desk to pay. If you weren't given a chit, you'll need to be able to quote the name of the item, the price (**цена́**/*tsena*) and the name or number of the department in the store (e.g. **второ́й отде́л**/*vtaroi atdyel*, second department). You'll then get a receipt (another **чек**).

**3 Collection** Take your receipt back to the first counter, and collect your purchases. In large department stores, you may have to do this at a central collection point (**вы́дача поку́пок**/*vydacha pakoopak*). Always keep your final receipt (**това́рный чек**/*tavarniy chek*) as you may need to show it at customs when leaving the country.

## в универмаге/at the department store

Lucy wants to buy something
Russian to wear. She goes into
GUM, where she sees some
peasant blouses on display in
Ladies Wear (**Жéнская
Одéжда**/*Zhenskaya Adyezhda*).

| | |
|---|---|
| Assistant: | **Что вам нýжно?** |
| | *Shto vam nuzhna?* |
| Lucy: | **Покажúте пожáлуйста** блýзку. |
| | *Pakazhitye pazhalasta bloozkoo.* |
| Assistant: | **Эту\* крáсную?** |
| | *Etoo krasnuyoo?* |
| Lucy: | **Нет, не ту\* — бéлую. Да, вот эту. Мóжно помéрить?** |
| | *Nyet, ni too — byeluyoo. Da, vot etoo. Mozhna pamyerit?* |
| Assistant: | **Да, конéчно. Какóй размéр?** |
| | *Da, kanyeshna. Kakoi razmer?* |
| Lucy: | **Я не знáю.** |
| | *Ya ni znayoo.* |
| Assistant: | **Дýмаю, что для вас эта годúтся.** |
| | *Doomayoo shto dlya vas eta gaditsa.* |

(Lucy goes into the changing room and tries the blouse on)

Lucy:     **Мне о́чень нра́вится э́та блу́зка.**
          **Вы́пишите чек**, пожа́луйста.
          *Mnye ochin nravitsa eta bloozka.*
          *Vypishitye chek, pazhalasta.*

Assistant:  С удово́льствием. Она́ на вас хорошо́
            сиди́т – краси́вая англича́нка!
            *S udavolstviyem. Ana na vas kharasho
            sidit – krasivaya anglichanka!*

**С удово́льствием**     With pleasure
**краси́вая англича́нка!**  beautiful English girl!

*** Э́ту** and **ту** are the accusative forms of **э́та** and **та** – see grammar note.

| | |
|---|---|
| **5. ЭТА́Ж** | рестора́н restaurant   де́тская оде́жда children's clothes   тка́ни fabrics |
| **4. ЭТА́Ж** | ме́бель furniture   электроприбо́ры electrical goods   кафе́ cafe |
| **3. ЭТА́Ж** | ку́хонная посу́да kitchenware   фарфо́р china   сувени́ры souvenirs |
| **2. ЭТА́Ж** | же́нская оде́жда ladies' wear   мужска́я оде́жда men's wear   о́бувь shoes |
| **1. ЭТА́Ж** | кни́ги books   ка́рты maps   духи́ perfumes   пла́тки scarves   зо́нтики umbrellas |

## Buying clothes

When buying clothes, or anything else for that matter, the easiest thing to do is simply to point to what you want and say **вот э́то**/*vot eta* (this one); if the assistant doesn't get it right at first, you can say **Нет, не э́то, а вот э́то**/*Nyet, ni eta a vot eta* (No, not this one – *this* one).

**Покажи́те пожа́луйста бе́лую блу́зку**
*Pakazhitye pazhalasta byeluyoo bloozkoo*

Show me the white blouse, please

**Не ту – да, вот э́ту**
*Ni too – da, vot etoo*

Not that one – yes, that's it

**Мо́жно поме́рить?**
*Mozhna pamyerit?*

Can I try it on?

**Како́й разме́р?**
*Kakoi razmyer?*

What size?

**Мо́жете ли вы снять с меня́ ме́рку?**
*Mozhetye li vy snyat s minya myerkoo?*

Can you measure me?

**Ду́маю, что э́та годи́тся**
*Dumayoo, shto eta gaditsa*

I think this one will do

**У вас есть то же пла́тье друго́го цве́та?**
*U vas yest to zhe platye drugova tsvyeta?*

Do you have this dress in another colour?

**Оно́ мне велико́/мало́**
*Ano mnye vyeliko/malo*

It's too big/small for me

**У вас есть что́-нибудь побо́льше/поме́ньше**
*U vas yest shto-niboot pabolshi/pamyenshi*

Have you anything bigger/smaller?

**Это сли́шком ко́ротко/дли́нно/те́сно**
*Eta slishkam koratka/dlinna/tyesna*

It's too short/long/tight

74

**Ту́фли сли́шком у́зки/широки́**
*Toofli slishkam oozki/shiraki*
**Мне о́чень нра́вится**
*Mnye ochin nravitsa*
**На вас хорошо́ сиди́т**
*Na vas kharasho sidit*
**Заверни́те, пожа́луйста**
*Zavirnitye, pazhalasta*
**Я про́сто смотрю́**
*Ya prosta smatryoo*

The shoes are too small/big

I like it very much

It fits you very well

Wrap it up, please

I'm just looking

## *the way it works*

### *This one and that one*

The word for 'this' used in a general way is **э́то**/*eta*. With a noun it's either:

| *masc.* | *fem.* | *neuter* | *plural* |
|---|---|---|---|
| **э́тот** пояс | **э́та** ю́бка | **э́то** пальто́ | **э́ти** брю́ки |
| *etat poyas* | *eta yoopka* | *eta palto* | *eti bryooki* |
| this belt | this skirt | this coat | these trousers |

The word for 'that' is **то**/*to*:

| *masc.* | *fem.* | *neuter* | *plural* |
|---|---|---|---|
| **тот** шарф | **та** шу́ба | **то** пла́тье | **те** носки́ |
| *tot sharf* | *ta shuba* | *to platye* | *tye naski* |
| that scarf | that fur coat | that dress | those socks |

When asking to buy things, for something to eat etc., you will often find the accusative case is used (e.g. I want *this blouse*, Give me *that pear*):

**Я хочу́ э́ту блу́зку**/*Ya khachoo etoo bluzkoo*
**Да́йте ту гру́шу**/*Daitye too grushoo*

### *If you haven't got any . . .*

After a negative statement, such as 'I haven't any . . .', 'there isn't any . . .' and so on, you will find the genitive case used in Russian. There are quite a few examples of this in the dialogues to date. Here are some more:

**У нас нет хле́ба/молока́/яиц**
*U nas nyet khlyeba/malaka/yaits*
**У вас есть де́ньги? – У меня́ нет де́нег**\*
*U vas yest dyengi? – U minya nyet dyenek.*
**У вас есть ме́лочь? – У меня́ нет ме́лочи.**
*U vas yest myelach? – U minya nyet myelachi.*

We haven't any
  bread/milk/eggs
Have you any money? –
  I have no money
Have you any change? –
  I haven't any change

\* **де́нег** is the genitive plural of **де́ньги** (money) and you will probably hear both words quite frequently!

## I like it, I don't like it

If you are talking about liking something specific, rather than in a general way, then use the expression **мне нра́вится**/*mnye nravitsa* (lit. it is pleasing to me):

**Э́та руба́шка мне о́чень нра́вится, ...**    I like this shirt very much ...
*Eta rubashka mnye ochin nravitsa ...*
**... а сви́тер мне совсе́м не нра́вится**    ... but I don't like the sweater at all
*... a sviter mnye savsyem ni nravitsa*

For words in the plural, use **мне нра́вятся**/*mnye nravyatsa*.

## things to do

**5.5**    You are buying food for a picnic and jot down a few of the things you need. How much money must you spend in order to buy these items: **пятьсо́т грамм помидо́ров, два кило́ я́блок, кило́ груш, пли́тка шокола́да?**

30 коп.    1.30 р./кило    80 коп.    1.50 р./кило    1 р./кило

**5.6**    **В бу́лочной**    You are feeling rather hungry and are tempted by the smells coming from a bakery. See if you can ask for what you want.

| | |
|---|---|
| Assistant: | **Что вам ну́жно?** |
| You: | (You want a round loaf) |
| Assistant: | **Ещё что́-нибудь?** |
| You: | (You'd like two bread rolls and a pastry) |

**5.7**    You go into a department store determined to buy something to wear. Can you talk to the assistant?

| | |
|---|---|
| Продавщица: | **Вы что-нибудь хоти́те?** |
| Вы: | (Ask her to show you the green shirt in the window) |
| Продавщица: | **Э́ту?** |
| Вы: | (No, not that one, the one next to it .. Ask her the price.) |
| Продавщица: | **Сто́ит два́дцать пять рубле́й.** |
| Вы: | (You won't take it, it's too expensive) |

**5.8**  You want to buy the items on the left, but which shops should you go to? Match up the goods with the shops on the right.

(a)  бакалея
(b)  дом обуви
(c)  булочная
(d)  аптека
(e)  молочная
(f)  ювелирный магазин

**5.9**  **Сколько они стоят?**  You point to various things you want to buy in a department store, and the assistant tells you the prices – but you're not sure you've heard correctly, so you ask her **Напишите, пожалуйста** (Please write it down). Can you match what she said (on the left) to what she writes (on the right)?

1  Стоит рубль пятьдесят копеек.
2  Стоят шестьдесят копеек.
3  Стоит пять рублей.
4  Стоит восемь рублей сорок копеек.

книга 5р
пластинка 1р. 50к
открытки 60к
счёт 8р. 40к

**5.10**  You have finally chosen these articles in the souvenir department as gifts to take home, and the assistant tells you to pay at the cash desk. Can you tell the cashier (a) the name of the department (b) the name of each item (c) the price?

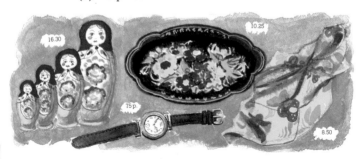

## MEDICAL PROBLEMS

If you fall ill in the Soviet Union, ask your hotel or Intourist Bureau to call the duty doctor. Medical treatment is free, though some medicines may not be. Hospital treatment will have to be paid for on the spot, so it's advisable to take out adequate medical insurance. Many Western medicaments simply do not exist, so if you rely on certain pills or medicines, don't forget to bring them with you. In Moscow, the special clinic for foreigners is at Gruzinsky Pereulok 3, Korpus 2.

The Russian health service runs on a system of polyclinics, and there are no GPs. However, Russians like to use herbal and simple home remedies for minor illnesses. Spas and health cure holidays combining sea or mountain air, mineral waters, physiotherapy etc. are extremely popular, and Intourist can arrange for tourists to take treatment at resort towns in the Caucasus or Crimea. Go to the chemist's for basic medicines such as aspirin (look for the sign **Дежу́рная Апте́ка**/*Dizhurnaya Aptyeka*, chemist's on rota), but do not expect to find an enormous range of toiletries – it's advisable to take such things as tampons and cosmetics with you.

# СУББОТА SATURDAY

## у меня простуда/I've got a cold

Mike Nash and his group have arrived in Yalta, where they are to spend the next two days at leisure on the Black Sea coast. Lena was hoping to organise an excursion in the afternoon, but unfortunately Mike isn't feeling too good …

Lena:  Что с ва́ми сего́дня, Майк? Вам пло́хо?
*Shto s vami sivodnya, Mike. Vam plokha?*

Mike:  Да, **я себя́ пло́хо чу́вствую. У меня́ боли́т** го́рло – и голова́. Ду́маю, что врач мне ну́жен.
*Da, ya sibya plokha choostvuyoo. U minya balit gorla – i galava. Dumayoo, shto vrach mnye nuzhen.*

Lena:  У вас есть температу́ра?
Э́то вероя́тно просту́да,
и́ли грипп. Пойдём
сперва́ в апте́ку.
*U vas yest timperatura?
Eta virayatna prastooda,
ili greep. Paeedyom
spirva v aptyekoo.*

| | | | |
|---|---|---|---|
| **Вам пло́хо?** | Aren't you well? | **врач** | doctor |
| **вероя́тно** | probably | **сперва́** | first of all |
| **У меня́ боли́т го́рло – и голова́** | I've got a headache – and a sore throat | | |

## в апте́ке/at the chemist's

Mike:  **У вас есть что́-нибудь от** гри́ппа?
*U vas yest shto-niboot at greeppa?*

Chemist:  Дава́йте посмо́трим … Вот – принима́йте э́ти табле́тки три ра́за в день, по́сле еды́.
*Davaitye pasmotrim … Vot – prinimaitye eti tabletki tree raza v dyen, posli yedy.*

Mike:  Спаси́бо. **Мо́жете дать мне та́кже** табле́тки для го́рла?
*Spaseeba. Mozhetye dat mnye takzhe tablyetki dlya gorla?*

Chemist:  К сожале́нию у меня́ нет табле́ток … а рекоменду́ю э́то но́вое полоска́ние для го́рла. У него́ о́чень прия́тный вкус!
*K sazhalyeniyoo u minya nyet tablyetak … a rikamyenduyoo eta novaye palaskaniye dlya gorla. U nyevo ochin priyatniy vkoos!*

| | |
|---|---|
| **что-нибу́дь от гри́ппа** | something for flu |
| **три ра́за** | 3 times |
| **полоска́ние** | gargle |
| **У него́ о́чень прия́тный вкус!** | It tastes very nice! |

## I don't feel very well

**Что с вáми ... вам плóхо?**
*Shto s vami ... vam plokha?*
What's the matter ... aren't you feeling well?

**Я плóхо/нехорошó чýвствую себя́**
*Ya plokha/nikharasho choostvuyoo sibya*
I feel ill

**Что у вас болúт?**
*Shto u vas balit?*
Where does it hurt?

**У меня́ болúт головá/гóрло/пáлец/зуб**
*U minya balit galava/gorla/palyets/zoop*
I've got a headache/sore throat/finger/tooth

**У меня́ простýда/температýра/грипп**
*U minya prastooda/timperatura/greep*
I've got a cold/ temperature/flu

**У меня́ запóр/понóс/несварéние желýдка**
*U minya zapor/panos/nisvaryeniye zheludka*
I've got constipation/ diarrhoea/indigestion

**меня́ тошнúт/меня́ рвёт**
*Minya tashnit/minya rvyot*
I feel sick/I've been sick

**У меня́ сóлнечный удáр/укýс насекóмого**
*U minya solnichniy udar/ukoos nasikomava*
I have sun stroke/an insect bite

**Я порéзал\* нóгу/обжёг рýку**
*Ya paryezal nogoo/abzhog rukoo*
I've cut my foot/burnt my hand

**У меня́ синя́к/порéз/растяжéние свя́зок**
*U minya sinyak/paryez/rastyazheniye svyazak*
I have a bruise/cut/sprain

**Я сломáл/сломáла себé ...**
*Ya slamal/slamala sibye ...*
I have broken ...

**Мне нýжен врач**
*Mnye nuzhen vrach*
I need a doctor

\* If it's a woman talking, you add **a** to the past tense endings: **я порéзала** ...
(see grammar section on p. 93 for more about the past tense).

See p. 115 for a list of parts of the body.

## Things the doctor should know

**Я астмáтик/диабéтик**
*Ya astmatik/diabetik*
I'm asthmatic/diabetic

**У меня́ сеннáя лихорáдка/больнóе сéрдце**
*U minya sinnaya likharadka/balnoye sertse*
I have hay fever/ heart trouble

**Я не переношý пенициллúн/антибиóтики**
*Ya ni pirinashoo pyenitsilin/antibiotiki*
I can't take penicillin/ antibiotics

**Я принимáю э́ти пилю́ли/таблéтки**
*Ya prinimayoo eti pilyooli/tablyetki*
I'm taking these pills/ tablets

**Я берéменна**
*Ya biryeminna*
I'm pregnant

**Я принимáю противозачáточные срéдства**
*Ya prinimayoo prativazachatachnye sredstva*
I'm on the pill

*At the chemist's*

**У вас есть что́-нибудь от гри́ппа/просту́ды/
тошноты́?**
*U vas yest shto-niboot at greeppa/prastudy/
tashnaty?*

Have you got something for
flu/cold/nausea?

**Принима́йте э́то лека́рство/э́ти табле́тки**
*Prinimaitye eta likarstva/eti tablyetki*

Take this medicine/these
tablets

**ка́ждые четы́ре часа́/три ра́за в день**
*kazhdye chetirye chasa/tree raza v dyen*

every four hours/three
times a day

**по ча́йной ло́жке/по́сле еды́, пе́ред едо́й**
*po chainoi lozhki/posli yedy, peryed yedoi*

one teaspoonful/after meals,
before meals

**Вам ну́жен врач**
*Vam nuzhen vrach*

You need a doctor

Here are some of the things you might want to buy at the chemist's:

| | |
|---|---|
| aspirin | **аспири́н**/*aspirin* |
| bandage | **бинт**/*bint* |
| contraceptives | **противозача́точное сре́дство**/*prativazachatachnaye sredstva* |
| cotton wool | **ва́та**/*vata* |
| gargle | **полоска́ние для го́рла**/*palaskaniye dlya gorla* |
| ointment | **мазь**/*maz* |
| plaster | **пла́стырь**/*plastyr* |
| insect repellent | **сре́дство от комаро́в**/*sredstva at kamarof* |
| laxative | **слаби́тельное**/*slabitelnaye* |
| throat tablets | **табле́тки для го́рла**/*tablyetki dlya gorla* |
| sanitary towels | **гигиени́ческие салфе́тки**/*gigienicheskiye salfyetki* |

АПТЕКА

For a list of toiletries, see p. 115.

# GETTING A SNACK/TALKING ABOUT
# THE WEATHER

## в закусочной/at the snack bar

On the way back from the chemist's, Lena begins to feel the pangs
of hunger. Although it's very hot and Mike still isn't well, she
persuades him to call in at a snack bar.

Lena:   Что вам уго́дно? Есть бутербро́ды с колбасо́й, с икро́й или
с сы́ром. У них та́кже пи́роги с ри́сом, с капу́стой или с
мя́сом.
*Shto vam ugodna? Yest booterbrody s kalbasoi, s ikroi ili s
syram. U nikh takzhe piragi s risam, s kapustoi ili s myasam.*

**Mike:** **Я совсём не голóден,** а мне óчень хóчется пить.
Сегóдня **так жáрко.**

*Ya savsyem ni galodyen, a mnye ochin khochitsa peet.*
*Sivodnya tak zharko.*

**Lena:** Да, **хорóшая погóда.** Сóлнце всегдá сийет здесь, дáже
зимóй. Мнóго людéй отдыхáют в Ялте! Но скажúте, Майк,
вы хорошó говорúте по-рýсски – вы родúлись в
Великобритáнии, прáвда?

*Da, kharoshaya pagoda. Sontsi vsikda siyaet zdyes, dazhe*
*zimoi. Mnoga lyoodyei atdykhayoot v Yalti! No skazhityte,*
*Mike, vy kharosho gavarityte pa-roosski – vy radilis v*
*Vyelikobritanii, pravda?*

**Mike:** Да, но у меня рýсская бáбушка – а моя женá америкáнка,
из Вашингтóна.

*Da, no u minya roosskaya babushka – a maya zhena*
*amerikanka, iz Vashingtona.*

**Lena:** Интерéсно! . . . Вот нáши напúтки. Давáйте вýпьем за
международную дрýжбу!

*Intiryesna! . . . Vot nashi napitki. Davaitye vypyem za*
*myezhdu-narodnuyoo druzhboo!*

| | | | |
|---|---|---|---|
| **я не голóден** | I'm not hungry | **мне хóчется пить** | I feel like drinking |
| **так жáрко** | it's so hot | **сóлнце** | the sun |
| **бáбушка,** | grandmother, | | |
| **женá** | wife | | |
| **Мнóго людéй отдыхáют в Ялте** | | Lots of people come on holiday to Yalta | |
| **Вы родилúсь . . ., прáвда?** | | You were born . . ., weren't you? | |
| **Давáйте вýпьем за международную** | | Let's drink to international | |
| **дрýжбу!** | | friendship! | |

If you're feeling hungry between meals, or you want a snack for
lunch, here are some of the things you might find at a cafe or snack
bar:

| | |
|---|---|
| **бутербрóд с колбасóй/с икрóй** | a salami/caviare sandwich |
| *booterbrod s kalbasoi/s ikroi* | |
| **пирожкú**/*pirazhki* | patties, stuffed dumplings |
| **сардéльки**/*sardyelki* | little sausages, frankfurters |
| **копчёная колбасá**/*kapchonaya kalbasa* | smoked sausage |
| **пирóг с мясом**/*pirog s myasam* | meat pie |
| **пирóг с рúсом/с капýстой**/*pirog s risam/* | rice/cabbage pie |
| *s kapustoi* | |
| **жáреная картóшка**/*zharinaya kartoshka* | chips |
| **сырники, олáдьи**/*syrniki, oladi* | cheese cakes, thick pancakes |

# СУББОТА  SATURDAY

▶ ▶ ▶ **Weather**  If you visit the Soviet Union between November and March, don't forget that it can be extremely cold. For outdoor wear you'll need a thick overcoat, warm gloves, and most important, a hat that covers your ears. Hotel rooms are usually well heated. In the South it may be warm from April onwards, and wherever you go you can expect a fair amount of hot, sunny weather from May to the end of August – but take your umbrella as there will almost certainly be the occasional summer shower.

## Какая сегодня погода? *What's the weather like today?*

| | |
|---|---|
| **хорóшая погóда/плохáя погóда** *xharoshaya pagoda/ploxhaya pagoda* | it's fine/it's bad weather |
| **жáрко/хóлодно** *zharka/kholadna* | it's hot/it's cold |
| **теплó/вéтрено** *tiplo/vetrino* | it's warm/it's windy |
| **сегóдня тумáн** *sivodnya tooman* | it's foggy today |
| **идёт дождь/снег** *idyot dozhd/snyek* | it's raining/snowing |
| **морóзит** *marozit* | it's freezing |
| **Сóлнце всегдá сиáет, дáже зимóй** *Sontsi vsikda siyaet, dazhe zimoi* | The sun always shines, even in winter |

## *Languages and nationalities*

| | |
|---|---|
| **Вы óчень хорошó говорúте по-рýсски/ по-англúйски** *Vy ochin kharasho gavarityе pa-roosski/ pa-angliski* | You speak Russian/English very well |
| **Вы родилúсь в Великобритáнии/США?** *Vy radilis v Vyelikobritanii/Say-Sha?* | Were you born in Great Britain/USA? |
| **Я англичáнин/англичáнка/американец/ американка** *Ya anglichanin/anglichanka/amerikanits/ amerikanka* | I'm English/American |

## *the way it works*

### У меня болит . . .

This expression means 'My . . . hurts'. If you want to say his, or her or their . . . hurts, you use **у негó**/*u nyevo*, **у неё**/*u nyeyo* or **у них**/*u nikh*:

**У негó болúт ногá**  *U nyevo balit naga*  His leg hurts/He has a sore leg

## 'Our' and 'their'

The word for 'our' is **наш** (*nash*). It works like **ваш**: **на́ши напи́тки**/*nashi napitki* (our drinks). If you want to say 'their', use **их**: **их заку́ски**/*ikh zakuski* (their snacks).

## Пиро́г с гриба́ми *Pie with mushrooms* (The instrumental case)

There are many uses for the instrumental case, the main one being to denote the instrument by means of which you do something, e.g.

**Я пишу́ ру́чкой**/*Ya pishoo ruchkoi* I write with a pen (**ру́чка** = pen)

This case is always used after **с**/*s* (with). You have already met all of these:

| *masc. (and neuter)* | *feminine* | *plural* |
|---|---|---|
| **с мя́сом**/*s myasam* | **с икро́й**/*s ikroi* | **с гриба́ми**/*s gribami* |

Other nouns take similar endings in the instrumental. Note that **с** is often used when we would say 'and', e.g. **мя́со с карто́шкой** (meat and potatoes), **хлеб с ма́слом** (bread and butter).

Pronouns in the instrumental are as follows: **мной, тобо́й, им, ей, на́ми, ва́ми, и́ми**. After prepositions, they are

| | | | | |
|---|---|---|---|---|
| **со* мной**/*sa mnoi* | with me | **с на́ми**/*s nami* | with us |
| **с тобо́й**/*s taboi* | with you | **с ва́ми**/*s vami* | with you |
| **с ним**/*s neem* | with him/it | **с ни́ми**/*s nimi* | with them |
| **с ней**/*s nyei* | with her/it | | |

*In some expressions **с** adds an **о**.

Here is another use of **с**:

**мы с ва́ми**/*my s vami* you and I **мы с Ма́йком**/*my s Mikam* Mike and I

The instrumental is also used after the prepositions **пе́ред**/*piryed* (before), **за**/*za* (behind) and **над**/*nad* (above, over).

## *things to do*

**6.1** You are taken ill on the beach, and the doctor doesn't seem to understand much English. Can you describe your symptoms?

| | |
|---|---|
| Врач: | Расскажи́те, что у вас боли́т? |
| Вы: | (You've got a stomach ache) |
| Врач: | Что ещё? |
| Вы: | (Yes, a headache and you feel sick) |
| Врач: | У вас высо́кая температу́ра – э́то вероя́тно со́лнечный уда́р. |

Did you understand the diagnosis?

**6.2** Various guests at your hotel are suffering from a number of ailments. Can you explain to the doctor what is the matter with each of them?

1 Joanna: she's got a sore foot.
2 Peter: he's got a bad back.
3 Cathy: indigestion.
4 Simon: an insect bite.
5 Julia: a cold.

**6.3** Now you've been sent to the chemist's to buy supplies for members of your group.

1  cotton wool, throat sweets and insect repellent.

2  some toothpaste, soap and razor blades.

3  something for diarrhoea.

**6.4** All that sea air has made you feel hungry, so you and a friend go into a cafe for a snack. Ask for the following:

cheese sandwich                    a caviare sandwich

a meat pie                         some cheese cakes

▶▶▶ **Asian USSR**   It is hard to believe that the Central Asian Soviet Republics are part of the same country as the Western Republics, as here are people with different features, in different dress and speaking different languages – and yet the official language is Russian, and you will find names of streets, shops, buildings etc. in Russian and the same type of municipal buildings and statues of Lenin that can be found all over the country, from Moscow to Vladivostock. With the Russian you have learnt, you will be able to make yourself understood wherever you go in the Soviet Union!

Tashkent, the capital of Uzbekistan, contains large modern hotels and modern blocks of flats, yet the Eastern customs prevail, and in the museums you will see oriental pottery and jewellery, splendid rugs and silks, and the distinctive colourful embroidery and embroidered skull-caps of the region.

## STAMPS AND POST OFFICES

### марки купить/buying stamps

After a lightning tour of the city on a wet morning, Lucy has bought some post cards with views of Tashkent. She goes along to the hotel kiosk for some stamps.

Lucy:    **Ско́лько сто́ит откры́тка в А́нглию,** пожа́луйста?
*Skolka stoit atkrytka v Angliyoo, pazhalasta?*

Assistant:    В А́нглию? Откры́тка сто́ит пятьдеся́т копе́ек.
*V Angliyoo? Atkrytka stoit pyatdisyat kapeyek.*

Lucy:    **Две ма́рки,** пожа́луйста, **и одну́ для письма́ в** Кана́ду.
*Dvye marki, pazhalasta, i adnoo dlya pisma v Kanadoo.*

Assistant:    Авиаписьмо́? Вот. Э́то сто́ит … (She adds up the amount. Lucy pays and turns to go) **Эй, девущка, не забу́дьте зо́нтик!**
*Aviapismo? Vot. Eta stoit … Ey, dyevushka, ni zabudtye zontik!*

| | | | |
|---|---|---|---|
| **две ма́рки** | two stamps | **письмо́** | a letter |
| **не забу́дьте зо́нтик** | don't forget your umbrella | | |

Lucy bought her stamps at the hotel kiosk, where they also sell postcards, writing paper (**почто́вая бума́га**/*pachtovaya bumaga*) and envelopes (**конве́рты**/*kanvyerty*). However, she might equally well have gone to the post office.

▶▶▶ **Post offices** offer postal, telegram, telephone and telex facilities, and are open from 9.00 am to 6.00 or 7.00 pm. As well as buying stamps etc., you can send international telegrams (look for the sign **Междунаро́дная Телегра́мма**, and pick up a form – **междунаро́дный бланк**/*mizhdunarodniy blank*). If you want to send a parcel home, hand over the *contents* to the counter clerk and ask him to wrap them (**Заверни́те**/*Zavirnitye*). Then your parcel will be weighed and stamped, you'll be asked to write your address on the back and given a receipt.

Many large hotels contain a branch of the post office on the premises, and most transactions can be conducted here fairly easily!

## На по́чте *At the post office*

**Где я могу́ купи́ть ма́рки?**
*Gdye ya magoo koopit marki?*

Where can I buy stamps?

**Вон там, в окне́ пять**
*Von tam, v aknye pyat*

Over there, at counter 5

**Ско́лько сто́ит откры́тка в А́нглию?**
*Skolka stoit atkrytka v Angliyoo?*

How much is a postcard to England?

**Ско́лько сто́ит письмо́ в Кана́ду?**
*Skolka stoit pismo v Kanadoo?*

How much is a letter to Canada?

**авиаписьмо́/посы́лка/перево́д**
*aviapismo/pasylka/pirivod*

an air letter/a parcel/money order

**Ма́рка за пятьдеся́т копе́ек**
*Marka za pyatdisyat kapeyek*

A 50 kopeck stamp

**Две ма́рки/Пять ма́рок за … копе́ек**
*Dvye marki/Pyat marak za … kapeyek*

Two/five stamps at … kopecks

**Я хочу́ посла́ть заказно́е письмо́**
*Ya khachoo paslat zakaznoye pismo*

I want to send a registered letter

**Где по́чта до востре́бования?**
*Gdye pochta da vastrebavaniya?*

Where is the poste restante counter?

**Где почто́вый я́щик?**
*Gdye pachtovy yashchik?*

Where's the postbox?

## MAKING A PHONE CALL

## разговор по телефону/telephone conversation

Meanwhile, there is something of a crisis in the hotel foyer, as Donald has discovered his wallet is missing. He thinks he may have left it in the Tea House they visited in the morning, so Vadim makes a quick phone call on his behalf. Having ascertained the number, he picks up the receiver and dials.

Vadim: **Ох, не отвеча́ют . . . а, вот кто-то!**
*Okh, ni atvyechayoot . . . a, vot kto-ta!*

Manager: **Алло́, слу́шаю.**
*Allo, slooshayoo.*

Vadim: **Алло́, э́то говори́т Ва́дим Иго́ревич Григо́ров.**
**Извини́те, ка́жется мы оста́вили у вас бума́жник сего́дня у́тром.**
*Allo, eta gavarit Vadim Igorevich Grigorov. Izvinitye, kazhitsa my astavili u vas bumazhnik sivodnya utram.*

Manager: **Подожди́те одну́ мину́точку . . . (returning) Алло́?**
**Мо́жете описа́ть бума́жник? Како́й цвет, наприме́р?**
*Padazhditye adnoo minutachkoo . . . Allo? Mozhetye apisat bumazhnik? Kakoi tsvyet, naprimer?*

# СУББОТА  SATURDAY

Vadim: **Это óчень большóй бумáжник, из корúчневой кóжи.**
*Eta ochen balshoi bumazhnik, iz karichnyevoi kozhi.*

Manager: **Óчень жаль. Кто-то остáвил у нас крáсную сýмочку, а бумáжников нет.**
*Ochin zhal. Kto-ta astavil u nas krasnuyoo sumachkoo, a bumazhnikof nyet*

Vadim: **Но – у Тóни крáсная сýмочка …!**
*No – u Toni krasnaya sumachka …!*

| | |
|---|---|
| **кáжется мы остáвили у вас бумáжник** | it seems we left a wallet at your place |
| **описáть** | describe |
| **напримéр** | for example |
| **из корúчневой кóжи** | in brown leather |
| **кто-то** | someone |
| **У Тóни крáсная сýмочка** | Tonya has a red handbag |

▶▶▶ **Using the telephone**  It's very cheap to make local phone calls in the Soviet Union. In large cities there are plenty of public phone boxes (**телефóн-автомáт**/*tilifon aftamat*) and the procedure is simple. Lift the receiver, insert 2 kopecks, wait for the dialling fone and dial the number (**нóмер**/*nomir*).

To phone inter-city or abroad you should either go to a post office (the sign to look for is **Междунарóдный телефóнный перегово́рный пункт**, international telephone call point) where you'll be directed to a cabin (**кабúна**/*kabina*) when your call eventually comes through, or make the call through your hotel.

## По телефону *On the phone*

| | |
|---|---|
| **Мне нужно позвонить в Англию/США** | I need to phone England/ |
| *Mnye nuzhna pazvanit v Angliyoo/Sayshah* | USA |
| **Можно позвонить? Мне нужен этот номер** | Can I make a phone call? |
| *Mozhna pazvanit? Mnye nuzhen etat nomir* | I need this number |
| **Я хочу звонить Вадиму/Лёне** | I want to phone Vadim/ |
| *Ya khachoo zvanit Vadimoo/Lenye* | Lena |
| **Его/её нет дома** | He/she's not at home |
| *Yevo/yeyo nyet doma* | |
| **Занято/Это ошибка** | It's engaged/It's the wrong |
| *Zanyata/Eta ashipka* | number |
| **Не отвечают** | There's no reply |
| *Ni atvyechayoot* | |
| **Вас просят к телефону** | You're wanted on the phone |
| *Vas prosyat k tilifonoo* | |
| **Алло, слушаю** | Hello, (I'm listening) |
| *Allo, slushayoo* | |
| **Кто говорит? Это Вадим говорит** | Who's speaking? This is |
| *Kto gavarit? Eta Vadim gavarit* | Vadim |
| **Подождите одну минуточку** | Hold the line a minute |
| *Padazhditye adnoo minutachkoo* | |

# EMERGENCIES

With any luck, your visit to the Soviet Union will be trouble free, and any minor problems will be sorted out by your guide or Intourist Bureau. If you are out and about on your own and you or a companion is involved in an accident, there is an emergency ambulance service to call, and if you have a car accident you should register it at once with the traffic police and obtain a written form for insurance purposes. Here are some expressions we hope you won't need to use:

## В случае крайней необходимости *In case of emergency*

| | |
|---|---|
| **На помощь!** | Help! |
| *Na pomashch* | |
| **Где ближайшее отделение милиции?** | Where's the nearest police |
| *Gdye blizhaisheye atdilyeniye militsii?* | station? |
| **Я потерял/потеряла бумажник** | I have lost my wallet |
| *Ya patiryal/patiryala bumazhnik* | |
| **часы/сумочку/билеты/кошелёк** | my watch/handbag/tickets/ |
| *chasy/sumachkoo/bilyety/kashelyok* | purse |
| **Я заблудился/заблудилась** | I'm lost |
| *Ya zabludilsa/zabludilas* | |
| **Позовите милицию/врача** | Call the police/a doctor |
| *Pazavitye militsiyoo/vracha* | |

# СУББОТА    SATURDAY

| | |
|---|---|
| **Пожа́рная охра́на** *Pazharnaya axhrana* | The fire-brigade |
| **Ско́рая по́мощь** *Skoraya pomashch* | First aid (ambulance) |
| **Держи́ во́ра!** *Dirzhi vora!* | Stop thief! |
| **Брита́нское посо́льство** *Britanskaye pasolstva* | British Embassy |
| **На́бережная Мори́са Торе́за 14** *Nabyerizhnaya Marisa Toreza 14* | 14 Maurice Thorez Embankment (address of the embassy in Moscow) |

## the way it works

### -то, -нибудь

These endings can be added to mean 'some ...' (**-то** is more specific, **-нибудь** is undiscriminating and has the sense 'someone/thing etc. or other'):

| | |
|---|---|
| **Кто-то**/*Kto-ta* | Someone |
| **Что́-нибудь**/*Shto-niboot* | Something |
| **Где-то**/*Gdye-ta* | Somewhere |

## Я должна звонить Ивану *I must phone Ivan* (The dative case)

This case is used when we would often say 'to', e.g.

**Я пишу́ Миха́илу**   *Ya pishoo Mikhailoo*   I am writing to Mikhail

Sometimes the 'to' is omitted in English:

| | |
|---|---|
| **Я звоню́ Ве́ре** *Ya zvanyoo Verye* | I am phoning (lit. 'to') Vera |
| **Я пишу́ Миха́илу письмо́** *Ya pishoo Mikhailoo pismo* | I am writing Mikhail a letter |

In this last sentence, the letter is the *direct object* and Mikhail is the *indirect object*. Many nouns in the dative case behave as follows:

| masc. | neuter | fem. | plural |
|---|---|---|---|
| телефо́ну | ме́сту | по́чте | бума́жникам |
| *tilifonoo* | *myestoo* | *pochtye* | *bumazhnikam* |

Masculine nouns ending in a soft sign and neuter nouns ending in **-e** take **-ю**: **по́лю**. Feminine nouns ending in a soft sign take **-и** and those ending in **-ия** change to **-ии**: **но́чи, ста́нции**. Feminine nouns ending in **-я** change to **-е**: **То́не**.

You will also find the dative used after these verbs:

**расска́зывать**/*raskazyvat* (to tell), **объясня́ть**/*abyisnyat* (to explain), **приноси́ть**/*prinasit* (to bring).

Adjectives in the dative end in **ому/ему** for masculine, **ой/ей** for feminine.

You already know some of the pronouns in the dative case. Here is the full list:

**мне**/*mnye* (to) me
**тебе́**/*tibye* (to) you
**ему́**/*yemoo* (**нему́** after a prep.) (to) him
**ей**/*yei* (**ней** after a prep.) (to) her

**нам**/*nam* (to) us
**вам**/*vam* (to) you
**им**/*im* (**ним** after a prep.) (to) them

The dative case is used after the prepositions **по**/*po* (along, by) and **к**/*k* (to, towards).

## Кажется

This means literally 'it seems', and you will hear it used quite a lot in Russian, often with the sense of 'apparently': **Ка́жется ва́жное лицо́**/*Kazhitsa vazhnaye litso*: Apparently it's an important person. **Ка́жется** is often used with **мне, вас**, etc.:

**Мне ка́жется, что ...**   *Mnye kazhitsa, shto ...*   It seems to me that ...

There are many other so-called impersonal expressions in Russian. Here are some more:

**Мне хо́лодно**
*Mnye kholadna*

I'm cold (lit. it is cold to me)

**Нам ску́чно**
*Nam skushna*

We're bored (lit. it's boring to us)

**Вам хо́чется обра́тно?**
*Vam khochitsa abratno?*

Do you feel like going back?

## *An introduction to the past tense*

You will have noticed the past tense endings in many of the phrases to date. To form the past tense, you simply remove the infinitive ending from a verb and substitute **л**/*l* (masculine), **ло**/*lo* (neuter), **ла**/*la* (feminine) or **ли**/*li* (plural):

**До́налд потеря́л бума́жник**
*Donald patiryal bumazhnik*

Donald lost his wallet

**То́ня оста́вила су́мочку в чайха́не**
*Tonya astavila sumachkoo v chaikhani*

Tonya left her bag in the teahouse

**Они́ звони́ли хозя́ину**
*Ani zvanili khazyainoo*

They phoned the manager

Some verbs have irregular past tense endings, e.g.

**идти́** (to go):     **шёл**/*shol*    **шло**/*shlo*     **шла**/*shla*     **шли**/*shli*
**мочь** (to be able):  **мог**/*mok*   **могло́**/*muglo*  **могла́**/*mugla*  **могли́**/*mugli*

You will probably hear the verb 'to be' (**быть**/*byt*) used in the past tense:

**он был**/*on byl*        he was        **оно́ бы́ло**/*ano byla*     it was
**она́ была́**/*ana byla*   she was       **они́ бы́ли**/*ani byli*     they were

## *things to do*

**6.5** You have various things to send home, so you go into a post office. Can you communicate in Russian?

1 You want to send a letter to England. Ask how much it is.
2 You want two stamps at 50 kopecks.
3 Tell the clerk you want to send an international telegram and ask for the form.
4 You want to have a parcel wrapped, and to know how much it costs. What do you say?

**6.6** Problems with the phone ...

1 You are sitting in your hotel lounge, when an employee comes up to you and says: **Вас про́сят к телефо́ну**. What's going on?
2 You rush to the phone, and this is what you hear: **Алло́, э́то Мари́на Петро́вна?** Assuming this isn't the case, what do you reply?
3 You decide to make a phone call home, and eventually you get through to the operator, who says: **Подожди́те одну́ мину́ту**. What is she telling you?

**6.7** Here are some of the things that Lucy's group have inadvertently mislaid. Can you say what each of them is in Russian? Begin: **Мы потеря́ли ...**

## SPORT AND LEISURE

▶▶▶ **Leisure activities**  There are plenty of opportunities to practise sport in the Soviet Union, as main cities have large modern sports centres, such as the Kirov Stadium in Leningrad or the Luzhniki Sports Centre in Moscow, with its skating rinks and tennis courts. You will find swimming pools everywhere, particularly open-air heated pools which are open summer and winter alike, and taking saunas is something of a national pastime. You can hire skis, sledges and skates for use in the Moscow and Leningrad parks and there is cross-country skiing around Moscow, but for more serious mountain skiing, you should join a trip to the Caucasus. Intourist also arranges hunting trips to the Caucasian mountains, Siberia and the Ukraine, with all equipment provided. Ice hockey (**хоккей**/*khakkei*) and football (**футбол**/*futbol*) are among the most popular games in the Soviet Union and athetics (**атлётика**/*atlietika*) has a large following. Tickets for football matches can be bought from the stadium, or in Moscow from Metro station kiosks.

▶▶▶ **Camping**  If you want to camp, you'll need to take a car. Camping is still very primitive and you won't find any luxury facilities. You will have to make arrangements in advance and pay with Intourist camping vouchers (**талóны**/*talony*). You can hire a tent, and at most camp-sites (**кемпинги**/*kempingi*) ready-cooked meals are available. Many sites are only open for three months in the summer.

# ВОСКРЕСЕНЬЕ SUNDAY

## у мо́ря/by the sea

Mike and Alice are up early on Sunday morning. It is a lovely day, the water looks inviting, and Mike is trying to persuade Lena to come for a swim.

Mike: **Смотри́те, сего́дня мо́ре тако́е споко́йное. Пойдём купа́ться!** Лё́на, у вас есть купа́льный костю́м?
*Smatritye, sivodnya morye takoye spakoinaye. Paeedyom koopatsa! Lyena, u vas yest koopalniy kastyoom?*

Lena: Я пло́хо пла́ваю, но **о́чень люблю́ игра́ть в** те́ннис. Вы лю́бите спорт? Здесь прекра́сные те́ннисные ко́рты ря́дом с гости́ницей – и́ли **мо́жно взять** ло́дки **напрока́т**.
*Ya plokha plavayoo, no ochin lublyoo igrat v tenis. Vy lyoobitye sport? Zdyes prikrasnye tennisnye korty ryadam s gastinitsei – ili mozhna vzyat lotki naprakat.*

Alice: **Мо́жно игра́ть в** волейбо́л на пля́же?
*Mozhna igrat v valyeibol na plyazhi?*

Lena: Да, коне́чно. Пойдёмте.
*Da, kanyeshna. Paeedyomtye.*

| мо́ре так споко́йно | the sea is so calm |
| Пойдём купа́ться! | Let's go for a swim! |
| у вас есть купа́льный костю́м | have you got a bathing costume? |
| взять ло́дки напрока́т | to hire boats |
| на пля́же | on the beach |

### What do you like playing?

**Здесь прекра́сные те́ннисные ко́рты**
*Zdyes prikrasnye tyennisnye korty*
**Я люблю́ игра́ть в** те́ннис/в хокке́й
*Ya lublyoo igrat v tenis/v xhakkei*
  **в футбо́л/в волейбо́л**
  *v futbol/v valyeibol*
**Я люблю́ спорт/гимна́стику/ры́бную ло́влю**
*Ya lublyoo sport/gimnastikoo/rybnuyoo lovlyoo*

There are good tennis courts here
I like playing tennis/ hockey
football/volleyball
I like sport/gymnastics/ fishing

**Мо́жно купа́ться/бе́гать**
*Mozhna koopatsa/byegat*
  **ходи́ть на лы́жах/ката́ться на конька́х**
  *xhadit na lyzhakh/katatsa na kankakh*
  **ката́ться на тро́йке/на велосипе́де**
  *katatsa na troiki/na vilasipyedi*
**Мо́жно поста́вить пала́тку**
*Mozhna pastavit palatkoc*
**Я пло́хо пла́ваю**
*Ya plokha plavayoo*
**Я не уме́ю игра́ть в ша́хматы**
*Ya ni umyeoo igrat v shakhmaty*

It's possible to bathe/run

  to go skiing/to go
  skating
  to go for a troika ride/
  bike ride
It's possible to pitch a tent

I can't swim very well

I don't know how to play
chess

*What can we hire?*

**Мо́жно взять напрока́т лы́жи/конькй/раке́тку**
*Mozhna vzyat naprakat lyzhi/kanki/rakyetkoo*
  **са́ни/гребну́ю ло́дку/па́русную ло́дку**
  *sani/gribnuyoo lotkoo/parusnuyoo lotkoo*
  **мячй/во́дные лы́жи/се́рфинг**
  *myachi/vodnye lyzhi/serfing*
**Ско́лько сто́ит в час?**
*Skolka stoit v chas?*

You can hire skis/skates/
  a racket
  a sledge/rowing boat/
  sail boat
  balls/water skis/
  a windsurfer
How much does it cost
  for an hour?

*The vocabulary of sport*

| | | | | |
|---|---|---|---|---|
| cup | **ку́бок**/*kubak* | team | **кома́нда**/*kamanda* |
| game | **игра́**/*igra* | player | **игро́к**/*igrok* |
| match | **матч**/*match* | win, victory | **побе́да**/*pabyeda* |

▶▶▶ **Visiting the Black Sea coast** The Black Sea is where Russians like to go on holiday – notably to the famous Caucasian health resort of **Sochi**, or to **Yalta** with its palm trees, white buildings and backdrop of mountains. From Yalta, you can take boat trips down the coast, or join excursions up into the mountains. A few miles along the coast is the palace of **Livadia**, once a residence of the Russian royal family, now a museum and art gallery. Trade Unions and workplaces have their own holiday camps for the benefit of their workers, children come here with school or Pioneer groups to summer camps and the better off come to spend the summer in their own dachas. Nowadays Black Sea resorts are also used for catering for foreign tourists, and the atmosphere is relaxed and friendly.

## MAKING FRIENDS

No trip to a country is complete without some kind of contact with its inhabitants. If you are on business, you will have plenty of opportunity to talk to Russians, but if you are on holiday you may have to make your own opportunities. Many Russians have studied English at school and will be glad to talk to you. If you are invited out or if you are going to visit Russian friends, it's a nice gesture to take a little gift, such as flowers. Other gifts you might like to bring from home as presents for your guide, for example, could be chocolates, cosmetics, perfume, books and magazines (nothing risqué!), records or souvenirs.

### приглашение/an invitation

The three have just arrived at the beach, when Lena unexpectedly bumps into an old friend, Olga, and her son Sasha.

Lena: Óльга, какóй сюрпрѝз – и Сáшенька! Вы здесь в óтпуске?
*Olga, kakoi syurpreez – i Sashinka! Vy zdyes v otpuski?*

Olga: Да, мы отдыхáем в Ялте.
*Da, my atdykhayem v Yalti.*

Lena: Хорошó вам! Майк, **разрешѝте предстáвить** стáрую подрýгу. Áлис, э́то Сáша. (to Olga) Майк учѝтель рýсского языкá.
*Kharasho vam! Mike, razrishitye predstavit staruyoo padrugoo. Alice, eta Sasha. Mike uchityel roosskava yazyka.*

| | |
|---|---|
| Olga: | Вы здесь в Ялте в пе́рвый раз?<br>*Vy zdyes v Yaltye v pyerviy raz?* |
| Mike: | Да, но я отдыха́л в Со́чи два го́да тому́ наза́д.<br>*Da, no ya atdykhal v Sochi dva goda tamoo nazat.* |
| Olga: | И как вам нра́вится?<br>*I kak vam nravitsa?* |
| Alice: | **Замеча́тельно!**<br>*Zamichatyelna!* |
| Olga: | **Кака́я симпати́чная де́вушка! Майк, Али́с, я хочу́ вас пригласи́ть к нам на у́жин сего́дня ве́чером. Согла́сны?**<br>*Kakaya simpatichnaya dyevushka. Mike, Alice, ya khachoo vas priglasit k nam na uzhin sivodnya vyecheram. Saglasny?* |

| | |
|---|---|
| Mike: | Большо́е спаси́бо. Мы с удово́льствием придём.<br>*Balshoye spaseeba. My s udavolstviyem pridyom.* |

*Making conversation*

| | |
|---|---|
| **О́льга, како́й сюрпри́з!**<br>*Olga, kakoi syurpreez* | Olga, what a surprise! |
| **Вы здесь в о́тпуске? – Хорошо́ вам!**<br>*Vy zdyes v otpuski? – Xharasho vam!* | Are you here on holiday? – How nice for you |
| **Как (ваши) дела́?**<br>*Kak (vashi) dyela?* | How are things? |
| **Хорошо́/норма́льно/ничего́/пло́хо**<br>*Kharasho/narmalna/nichevo/plokha* | Fine/OK/not bad/not too good |
| **Разреши́те предста́вить ста́рую подру́гу**<br>*Razrishitye predstavit staruyoo padrugoo* | Let me introduce an old friend (female) |
| **Познако́мьтесь**<br>*Paznakomtyes* | Let's introduce ourselves |
| **Али́с, э́то Са́ша . . . о́чень рад/ра́да/ра́ды**<br>*Alice, eta Sasha . . . ochin rad/rada/rady* | Alice, this is Sasha . . . pleased to meet you |
| **Расскажи́те о себе́**<br>*Raskazhiti o sibye* | Tell me about yourself |
| **Вы здесь в пе́рвый раз?**<br>*Vy zdyes v pyerviy raz?* | Are you here for the first time? |
| **Отдыха́л в Крыму́ два го́да тому́ наза́д**<br>*Atdyxhal v Krymoo dva goda tamoo nazat* | I had a holiday in the Crimea 2 years ago |
| **Как вам нра́вится? – Замеча́тельно!**<br>*Kak vam nravitsa? – Zamichatyelna!* | How do you like it? – It's great! |

## Inviting someone round

**Я хочу́ пригласи́ть вас к нам на у́жин**
*Ya khachoo priglasit vas k nam na uzhin*
I want to invite you to supper with us

**Приходи́те к нам обе́дать/у́жинать**
*Prikhaditye k nam abyedat/uzhinat*
Come and have lunch/supper with us

**Приглашу́ вас на вечери́нку**
*Priglashoo vas na vyecherinkoo*
I'm inviting you to a party

**непреме́нно/согла́сны**
*nyeprimyenna/soglasny*
certainly/agreed

**Мы придём с удово́льствием**
*My pridyom s oodavolstviyem*
We'd love to come

**Кака́я симпати́чная да́ма!**
*Kakaya simpatichnaya dama!*
What a nice lady!

## Talking about jobs

**Чем вы занима́етесь?**
*Chem vy zanimaetyes?*
What do you do?

**Кем вы рабо́таете?**
*Kyem vy rabotaetye?*
What work do you do?

If you fall into conversation with Soviet citizens, you will want to be able to say whether you're here on business (**по дела́м**/*po dyelam*) or on holiday (**в о́тпуске**/*v otpuski*) and what you do for a living:

**Я коммерса́нт**
*Ya kammirsant*
I'm a businessman

**Я журнали́ст**
*Ya zhurnalist*
I'm a journalist

**Майк учи́тел**
*Mike uchityel*
Mike's a teacher

See p. 115 for a list of jobs.

## the way it works

### I play tennis

Use the expression **игра́ть в**/*igrat v* when talking about what games you play:

**Я игра́ю в те́ннис, в ка́рты**
*Ya igrayoo v tennis, v karty*
I play tennis, cards

If it's a musical instrument, you use **игра́ть на**/*igrat na*:

**Я игра́ю на пиани́но, на кларне́те, на скри́пке**
*Ya igrayoo na pianina, na klarnyeti, na skripki*
I play the piano, clarinet, violin

things to do

**7.1** This is something of a revision exercise – look back through earlier sections if you get stuck.

You feel like a swim so you head for the swimming bath (**бассе́йн для пла́вания**/*bassein dlya plavaniya*). See if you can cope with the cashier:

Вы: (You want to know how much it costs to get in)

Касси́р: **Сто́ит два рубля́.**

Вы: (You want to know what time the bath closes.)

Касси́р: **В полови́не седьмо́го.**

Вы: (You didn't bring a towel – can you have one?)

Касси́р: **Да, сто́ит ещё 50 копе́ек.**

Вы: (Tell him you're giving him 5 roubles)

Касси́р: **И вот вам сда́ча – 2 р. 50 коп. Спаси́бо.**

(**сда́ча** = change)

**7.2** You're interested in sport, so you go along to the local Sports Complex and look at the list of summer events.

**Ле́тние Собы́тия**
*Ку́бок Сове́тского Сою́за* (*All-Soviet Cup*)

| | |
|---|---|
| Вече́рняя Гимна́стика | 1 А́ВГУСТА |
| ЧЕМПИОНА́Т ЕВРО́ПЫ – А́тлетика | 15 А́ВГУСТА 14 ч. |
| Футбо́льный Матч СССР – ЧССР | 22 А́ВГУСТА 15 ч. |
| БОКС – Чемпиона́т СССР | 3 СЕНТЯБРЯ́ 17.30 ч. |

*Прода́жа биле́тов в Спорти́вном Ко́мплексе*

1 What could you go to on 22 August?
2 You are an Athletics fan. What is there to interest you?
3 At what sort of time can you see gymnastics?
4 What other championship is going to be on, and when?
5 Where can you get tickets for these events?

**7.3** Here are some of the things you and your friends would like to hire during your leisure time in the Soviet Union. Practise asking for them, and asking how much they will cost.

1

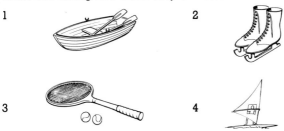

2

3

4

**7.4** You and a friend are sitting at a cafe on the sea front, and fall into conversation with a Russian lady on the next table. Can you make yourself understood? You have indicated that you're English. Now continue ..

| | |
|---|---|
| Дама: | Вы англичáне, вот интерéсно. Где вы живёте в Áнглии? |
| Вы: | (You're from London) |
| Дама: | Как вам нрáвится Крым? Здесь жáрко, не прáвда ли? |
| Вы: | (You like it very much, and yes it's very hot) |
| Дама: | Скажúте, кем вы рабóтаете? |
| Вы: | (Tell her what you do, e.g. you're a teacher and your friend is a doctor) |

# GOING ON AN EXCURSION

If you are on an organised holiday, you will be taken on at least one sightseeing tour, and will have the opportunity of joining the various excursions that are available in the Soviet Union. Excursions can only be undertaken with special permission, so if there is anything you particularly want to see, you should arrange it in writing beforehand, or apply to the Service Bureau at your hotel for advice.

There are many churches in the Soviet Union, and most of them are open to the public. The majority are now museums and have been beautifully restored or kept up. The country is proud of its ancient monuments and historic buildings and looks after them with care – visitors should do the same. In the churches in which services (**слу́жба**/*sluzhba*) are still held, you should behave respectfully, and women should wear headscarves.

# ВОСКРЕСЕНЬЕ SUNDAY

## экскурсия в древний город/an excursion to an ancient town

▶ ▶ ▶ **Samarkand**, once capital of the Mongol Empire, is a feast for the eye with its glorious mosques and many blue-tiled domes. Visitors flock to see the mausoleum of Gur Emir, Bibi Khanum's Mosque and the picture-book buildings of the Registan – once a theological college, now a showpiece of Eastern-style architecture.

Lucy and her fellow-travellers have arrived in Samarkand and spent the morning looking round the Registan complex. Vadim reminds them that an excursion has been planned for the afternoon ...

Vadim: Сегодня большая экскурсия в древний город, недалеко от Самарканда. Вы можете посмотреть чудесные минареты, мечеть четырнадцатого века с синей черепицей, мавзолей и памятники древней узбекской архитектуры. Автобус отправляется в два часа. Это вам подходит?

*Sivodnya balshaya ekskursiya v drevniy gorat, nidalyeko at Samarkanda. Vy mozhetye pasmatryet chudyesnye minarety, michet chetyrnatsatava vyeka s sinyei chirepitsei, mavzolei i pamyatniki drevnei uzbekskoi arkhitektury. Avtobus atpravlyaitsa v dva chasa. Eta vam padkhodit?*

Lucy: Да, восточная архитектура – очаровательна. Я должна вставить плёнку в фотоаппарат.

*Da, vastochnaya arkhitektura – acharavatilna. Ya dulzhna vstavit plyonkoo v fotoapparat.*

| | |
|---|---|
| мечеть | mosque |
| век | century |
| с синей черепицей | with blue tiles |
| памятники древней узбекской архитектуры | monuments of ancient Uzbek architecture |
| восточная | Eastern |
| вставить плёнку в | put a film in |

104

They arrive at the ancient city, and enter a mosque. Lucy is fascinated by the decorated ceiling, and the costumes of some of the women standing by the door.

Lucy: **Какóй удивительный потолóк, и какие прекрáсные костюмы! Я должнá дéлать снимки.**
*Kakoi udivityelniy patalok, i kakiye prekrasnye kastyoomy! Ya dulzhna dyelat snimki.*

(She gets out her camera and takes aim …)

Woman: **Нельзя фотографировать, как вам не стыдно!**
*Nilzya fatagrafiravat, kak vam ni stydna!*

Lucy: (Taken aback) **Виновáта, простите меня.**
*Vinavata, prastitye minya.*

Vadim: **Это не вáжно, Люси. Порá обрáтно – пойдём, выпем что-нибýдь холбдное в гостинице!**
*Eta ni vazhna, Lucy. Para abratna – paeedyom, vypyem shto-niboot khalodnaye v gastinitsi!*

| | |
|---|---|
| **Как вам не стыдно!** | Aren't you ashamed! |
| **простите меня** | excuse me |
| **Порá обрáтно** | It's time to get back |
| **Виновáта** | I'm sorry (fem.) |
| **не вáжно** | It's not important |

## *Taking a trip*

**Сегóдня экскýрсия в дрéвний гóрод**
*Sivodnya ekskursiya v drevniy gorat*
**в Бухáру/Петродворéц/Кремль**
*v Bukharoo/Petradvaryets/Kreml*
**посещéние музéя**
*pasyeshcheniye muzeya*

Today there's an excursion to an ancient town
to Bukhara/Petrodvorets/ the Kremlin
a visit to the museum

**Вы мóжете посмотрéть чудéсные минарéты**
*Vy mozhetye pasmatryet chudyesnye minarety*
**мечéть четырнадцатого вéка, мавзолéй**
*michet chetyrnatsatova vyeka, mavzolei*

You can see wonderful minarets
a 14th century mosque, a mausoleum

**посмотрéть Москвý/Киев/Новосибирск**
*pasmatryet Maskvoo/Kiev/Navasibirsk*
**Мóжно осмотрéть все достопримечáтельности**
*Mozhna asmatryet vsye dastaprimechatilnasti*

look at Moscow/Kiev/ Novosibirsk
You can see all the sights

**Автобус отправляется в два часа**
Avtobus atpravlyaitsa v dva chasa
**Это вам подходит?**
*Eta vam padkhodit?*
**восточная архитектура очаровательна**
*vastochnaya arkhitektura acharavatyelna*
**Какой удивительный потолок**
*Kakoi udivityelny patalok*

The coach sets off at
  2 o'clock
Does that suit you?

Eastern architecture is
  fascinating
What an amazing
  ceiling

For a list of places to see and things to look at, see p 116.

## TAKING PHOTOGRAPHS

Be careful how you aim your camera, as there are quite a number of places you are not allowed to photograph in the Soviet Union, among them airports, stations, military buildings etc., aerial views (e.g. from the top of a church or tower), bridges, border areas, industrial installations, the inside of shops and churches. Don't try to snap people in uniform or buildings where there is a uniformed guard. People at work don't generally like to be photographed, whether driving a bus or cleaning a building, and if you want to take a picture of someone, it is polite to ask for permission: **Можно вас фотографировать?**/ *Mozhna vas fatagrafiravat?* You can now buy colour film in some Beriozka shops, but as 35mm film is not readily available it is best to take your own supply.

### I must take a photo!

You'll want to take photos as a reminder of your trip, but don't do what Lucy did – remember to ask first!

**плёнка, цветная позитивная**
*plyonka, tsvitnaya pozitivnaya*
**Я должна вставить плёнку в фотоаппарат**
*Ya dulzhna vstavit plyonkoo v fotaapparat*
**... делать снимки**
*... dyelat snimki*
**Нельзя фотографировать**
*Nilzya fatagrafiravat*
**ФОТОГРАФИРОВАТЬ ЗАПРЕЩАЕТСЯ**
*Fatagrafiravat zaprishchaitsa*

film (colour slide)

I must put a film in my
  camera
... take some snaps

You can't take a photo

NO PHOTOGRAPHS

## the way it works

*Nouns and adjectives in Russian and how they work:*
*a résumé*

|  | *masc. sing.* |  | *masc. plural.* |  |
|---|---|---|---|---|
| Nominative: | белый стол | рубль | новые столы | рубли |
| Accusative: | белый стол | рубль | новые столы | рубли |
| Genitive: | белого стола | рубля | новых столов | рублей |
| Dative: | белому столу | рублю | новым столам | рублям |
| Instrumental: | белым столом | рублем | новыми столами | рублями |
| Locative: | белом столе | рубле | новых столах | рублях |

|  | *fem. sing* |  |  |  | *fem. plural* |  |  |
|---|---|---|---|---|---|---|---|
| Nominative: | старая | страна | дверь | земля | страны | двери | земли |
| Accusative: | старую | страну | дверь | землю | страны | двери | земли |
| Genitive: | старой | страны | двери | земли | стран | дверей | земель |
| Dative: | старой | стране | двери | земле | странам | дверям | землям |
| Instrumental: | старой | страной | двеью | землей | странами | дверями | землями |
| Locative: | старой | стране | двери | земле | странах | дверях | землях |

|  | *neuter sing.* |  | *neuter plural* |  |
|---|---|---|---|---|
| Nominative: | новое место | поле | места | поля |
| Accusative: | новое место | поле | места | поля |
| Genitive: | нового места | поля | мест | полей |
| Dative: | новому месту | полю | местам | полям |
| Instrumental: | новым местом | полем | местами | полями |
| Locative: | новом месте | поле | местах | полях |

Most nouns and adjectives in Russian follow similar patterns to these
(remember that after **г**, **к**, **х**, **ж**, **ч**, **ш** and **щ**, **ы** becomes **и**).

## things to do

**7.5**  You had a memorable time in the USSR. You're back home, and
tidying away some papers, when you come across the itinerary for
your trip. Here is the relevant page from your diary. Can you still
remember it all . . . ?

РАСПИСАНИЕ ПОЕЗДКИ
Пн.  Прибытие в Москву
     Посещение города –
     Кремль, Мавзолей Ленина
Вт.  Конференция
Ср.  Конференция
     Посещение ВДНХ*
Чт.  Экскурсия в Архангельское
     цена 25 р.

Пт.  Конференция
     Экскурсия в монстырь
     14-ого века ц. 15 р.
Сб.  Свободный день
     Вечеринка 20 ч.
Вс.  Отправление 12 ч.
     Москва-Шереметьево

\* **ВДНХ**: (Permanent) Exhibition of Economic Achievements of the USSR.

| | |
|---|---|
| **Mon** | Exhausting day, but memorable. Used up a whole film! |
| **Tues** | Hard at work today — made quite a few contacts. |
| **Wed** | Begining to get settled in. Particulary impressed by afternoon visit. |
| **Thurs** | A great day out. Made a new friend on the coach! |
| **Fri** | Last day on official business. Once again, interesting afternoon. |
| **Sat** | Went shopping, bought lots of presents and spent far too much money. The vodka flowed well into the night! |
| **Sun** | Flight was late, I think. Can't remember much about today... |

1  Why was Monday so exhausting, and what did you take pictures of?
2  What did you have to do on Tuesday, Wednesday and Friday?
3  Where did you go on Thursday? Was it free, or did you have to pay?
4  What excursion was available on Friday afternoon?
5  What was arranged for Saturday? What was arranged for the evening?
6  What time did you leave Moscow on Sunday?

# KEY TO EXERCISES

**Before you leave** 1 *kamyeta* (comet), *kafé* (café), *bolt* (bolt), *dama* (lady), *fakt* (fact), *kofi* (coffee), *balyet* (ballet), *mama* (Mummy), *ballada* (ballad), *takt* (tact), *foto* (photo), *koma* (coma), *tabak* (tobacco), *data* (data), *blok* (bloc), *katlyeta* (cutlet), *atam* (atom), *kadyet* (cadet). 2 *da*, *kto*, *eta*, *tyela*, *dom*, *kak*, *malako*, *moda*, *dyela*, *tam*, *tak*, *mala*. 3 *Taksi* (taxi), *tilifon* (telephone), *vistibyool* (vestibule), *traktor* (tractor), *park* (park), *viza* (visa), *toorist* (tourist), *tsentr* (centre), *klinik* (clinic), *boofyet* (buffet), *dinama* (dynamo), *kantsert* (concert), *film* (film), *bank* (bank), *mitro* (metro), *vino* (wine), *vodka* (vodka), *twalyet* (toilet), *stoodyent* (student), *gazyeta* (newspaper).

**1.1** 1 *ristaran* – restaurant
2 *intoorist* – Intourist
3 *sooveniry* – souvenirs
4 *kassa* – cash desk.
**1.2** 1 Здравствуйте. Очень приятно. 2 Добрый день.
3 Доброе утро. 4 До свидания.
**1.3** 2 Да, я мистер Наш. 3 Да, меня зовут Кларк. 4 Нет, меня зовут Томпсон. 5 Я Анна Блак/Меня зовут Анна Блак.
**1.4** 1 (Триста) пять, восемь и десять. 2 (Извините, пожалуйста) Где ванная? 3 Принесите мне полотенце.
**1.5** On the first floor; the snack bar.
**1.6** *kantora*, *zvanok*, *moozhskoi*, *zhenskiy*.
**1.7** 1 У вас есть чай с лимоном? 2 Дайте кофе и яблочный сок. 3 Бутылка лимонада, пожалуйста. Спасибо.
**1.8** Чашка кофе и стакан чая, пожалуйста./(Чай) Без сахара./У вас есть томатный сок?/Спасибо, нет. Дайте фруктовый сок, пожалуйста./Да, это всё. Спасибо.

**2.1** Fried eggs, jam.
**2.2** Я возьму/Дайте омлет./Омлет с ветчиной./Чай, пожалуйста.

**2.3** английская ... стоит ... рубль ... копеек ... журнал ... американский ... карту ... по-русски ... рубля. (Customer/News vendor: Good afternoon. Have you got an English paper?/Yes, I've got *The Times*./How much is it?/1 rouble 20 kopecks./I want to buy an English magazine too./I'm very sorry (I haven't got one). We've got an American magazine – *Time*./Give me a map of Leningrad./A map in Russian or in English?/In Russian, thank you./2 roubles 10 kopecks.
**2.4** 1 Стоит два рубля двадцать пять копеек. 2 Стоит один рубль десять копеек. 3 Стоит пятьдесят копеек. 4 Стоит два рубля пять копеек.
**2.5** *Kafé-Marozhenaye, Shashlychnaya, Zakoosachnaya.*
**2.6** Girl: Красная икра, баранина с рисом, компот. Man: Щи, котлеты по-киевски, ванильное мороженое. Man: Салат из помидоров, гуляш с картофелем, сыр. Lucy: Осетрина, свинина с грибами, кисель.
**2.7** Принесите/Дайте бутылку белого вина, джин с тоником, светлое пиво и водку.

**3.1** *Vkhod, Vykhad, Zapasnoi Vykhad, Vkhoda nyet, Vykhada nyet.*
**3.2** 3.
**3.3** 0.30 am; 12.30 pm; 17.40 pm; Это прямой поезд.
**3.4** Это место занято?/Можно открыть окно?/(Когда) В котором часу приходит поезд в Киев?/Пожалуйста, где вагон-ресторан?
**3.5** 1 В Лондоне, половина первого; в Москве, половина четвёртого. 2 В Москве, четверть двенадцатого; в Иркутске, четверть пятого. 3 В Нью-Йорке, пять часов; в Ленинграде, два часа. 4 В Ялте, без четверти семь; в Ташкенте, без четверти девять.

# KEY TO EXERCISES

**3.6** *stoitye* (wait, lit. stand), *iditye* (cross, lit. go), *stop* (stop), *pirikhod* (crossing), *byeregis aftamabilya* (beware of cars).
**3.7** (a) e.g. 1 Пожалуйста, где кино? 2 Как пройти в гостиницу?
3 Где находится стадион?
(b) 1 Bank. 2 Art gallery.
3 Museum.
**3.8** Hotel National, Lenin Museum, Red Square.

**4.1** *Kievskaya, Arbatskaya, Krapotkinskaya. Bibliotyeka im. (imyeni), Lenina, Ploshchad Sverdlova; apoostitye pyat kapeyek* – insert 5 kop., *k payezdam* – to the trains, *vykhad v gorad* – exit to the town.
**4.2** (a) 3, (b) 5, (c) 4, (d) 2, (e) 1.
**4.3** 1 Извините пожалуйста, где станция метро? 2 Извините пожалуйста, (вы не знаете) где станция Проспект Маркса?
3 Пожалуйста, где остановка троллейбуса? 4 В театр, пожалуйста. 5 Сорок литров, пожалуйста.
**4.4** *foyé* (foyer), *kooritelnaya komnata* (smoking room), *nilzya koorit v kino* (no smoking in the cinema), *administrator* (manager).
**4.5** 1. Yes. 2 Yes. 3 Mondays.
**4.6** 1 13th June 1989. 2 Dress circle, on the left. 3 Row 8, seat 5.
**4.7** 1 Два билета на балконе на завтра. 2 В котором часу начинается спектакль/ представление? 3 Один билет в партере – середина – на сегодня (вечером). 4 У вас есть места на сегодняшний концерт? 5 У меня оста́лось только билеты на седьмое февраля.

**5.1** 1 Можно обменять американские доллары?
2 Можно обменять двадцать пять фунтов? 3 Здесь можно разменять дорожные чеки?
4 Какой сегодня курс?
**5.2** (b).
**5.3** (c).
**5.4** мороженое – два,

пожалуйста; фруктовый сок – четыре, пожалуйста; билет – шесть, пожалуйста; открытки – десять, пожалуйста.
**5.5** 5 roubles 10 kopecks (пять рублей десять копеек).
**5.6** (Дайте) Батон, пожалуйста./ Две булочки и пирожное.
**5.7** Покажите пожалуйста зелёную рубашку в витрине./ Нет, не эту, а ту, рядом ... Сколько она стоит?/Нет, не надо – она слишком дорога.
**5.8** 1 (c), 2 (e), 3 (a), 4 (f), 5 (d), 6 (b).
**5.9** 1 Пластинка (the record).
2 Открытки (the postcards).
3 Книга (the book). 4 Счёт (the abacus).
**5.10** (a) Сувениры.
(b) & (c) Поднос, десять рублей двадцать пять копеек; шаль, восемь рублей пятьдесят копеек; часы, семьдесят пять рублей; матрёшка, шестнадцать рублей тридцать копеек.

**6.1** У меня болит желудок./Да, у меня болит голова, и меня тошнит. Diagnosis: sunstroke.
**6.2** 1 У неё болит нога. 2 У него болит спина. 3 У неё несварение желудка. 4 У него укус насекомого. 5 У неё простуда.
**6.3** 1 Вата, таблетки для горла, средство от комаров. 2 Зубная паста, мыло и лезвия. 3 У вас есть что-нибудь от поноса?
**6.4** Бутерброд с сыром; бутерброд с икрой; пирог с мясом; сырники.
**6.5** 1 Сколько стоит письмо в Англию? 2 Две марки за пятьдесят копеек. 3 Дайте мне/Где международный бланк?
4 Заверните, пожалуйста. Сколько стоит (посылка)?
**6.6** 1 You're wanted on the phone. 2 Нет, это ... (your name)/Это ошибка. 3 Hold the line a minute. 4 Go ahead and speak.

**6.7** Сумочку; фотоаппарат; паспорт; багаж; деньги.

**7.1** Пожалуйста, сколько стоит билет?/В котором часу закрывается бассейн?/(У вас есть) Можно взять напрокат полотенце?/Вот (вам) пять рублей.

**7.2** 1 Football match (USSR v. Czechoslovakia). 2 European championship on 15 August. 3 In the evening. 4 Boxing, on 3rd September at 5.30 pm. 5 At the sports complex.

**7.3** Я хочу/хотел бы/хотела бы взять напрокат гребную лодку ... коньки ... ракетку и мячи ... серфинг. Сколько стоит?

**7.4** (Я) Мы из Лондона./(Мне) нам очень нравится. Да, очень жарко./e.g. Я – учитель, мой друг (моя подруга) – врач.

**7.5** 1 You arrived in Moscow and then went on a visit of the city. You took pictures, among other things, of the Kremlin and Lenin's tomb. 2 You attended a conference. 3 You went to Archangelskoye and it cost you 25 roubles. 4 An excursion to a 14th century monastery. 5 It was a free day, with a party arranged for the evening. 6 You left at 12 midday.

# VOCABULARY

## Some common verbs in Russian

**дава́ть   to give**

| | | | | |
|---|---|---|---|---|
| я даю́/*ya dayoo* | I give | мы даём/*my dayom* | we give |
| ты даёшь/*ty dayosh* | you give | вы даёте/*vy dayotye* | you give |
| он даёт/*on dayot* | he gives | они́ даю́т/*ani dayoot* | they give |

**ви́деть   to see**

| | | | |
|---|---|---|---|
| я ви́жу/*ya vizhoo* | I see | мы ви́дим/*my vidim* | we see |
| ты ви́дишь/*ty vidish* | you see | вы ви́дите/*vy viditye* | you see |
| он ви́дит/*on vidit* | he sees | они́ ви́дят/*ani vidya* | they see |

**хоте́ть   to want**

| | | | |
|---|---|---|---|
| я хочу́/*ya khachoo* | I want | мы хоти́м/*my khatim* | we want |
| ты хо́чешь/*ty khochesh* | you want | вы хоти́те/*vy khatitye* | you want |
| он хо́чет/*on khochet* | he wants | они́ хотя́т/*oni khatyat* | they want |

**жить   to live, stay (in a hotel)**

| | | | |
|---|---|---|---|
| я живу́/*ya zhivoo* | I live | мы живём/*my zhivyom* | we live |
| ты живёшь/*ty zhivyosh* | you live | вы живёте/*vy zhivyotye* | you live |
| он живёт/*on zhivyot* | he lives | они́ живу́т/*ani zhivoot* | they live |

**мочь   to be able**

| | | | |
|---|---|---|---|
| я могу́/*ya magoo* | I can | мы мо́жем/*my mozhem* | we can |
| ты мо́жешь/*ty mozhesh* | you can | вы мо́жете/*vy mozhetye* | you can |
| он мо́жет/*on mozhet* | he can | они́ мо́гут/*ani mogoot* | they can |

**люби́ть   to like, love**

| | | | |
|---|---|---|---|
| я люблю́/*ya looblyoo* | I love | мы лю́бим/*my lyoobim* | we love |
| ты лю́бишь/*ty lyoobish* | you love | вы лю́бите/*vy lyoobitye* | you love |
| он лю́бит/*on lyoobit* | he loves | они́ лю́бят/*ani loobyat* | they love |

**писа́ть   to write**

| | | | |
|---|---|---|---|
| я пишу́/*ya pishoo* | I write | мы пи́шем/*my pishem* | we write |
| ты пи́шешь/*ty pishesh* | you write | вы пи́шете/*vy pishetye* | you write |
| он пи́шет/*on pishet* | he writes | они́ пи́шут/*ani pishoot* | they write |

**пить   to drink**

| | | | |
|---|---|---|---|
| я пью/*ya pyoo* | I drink | мы пьём/*my pyom* | we drink |
| ты пьёшь/*ty pyosh* | you drink | вы пьёте/*vy pyotye* | you drink |
| он пьёт/*on pyot* | he drinks | они́ пьют/*ani pyoot* | they drink |

**есть   to eat**

| | | | |
|---|---|---|---|
| я ем/*ya yem* | I eat | мы еди́м/*my yedim* | we eat |
| ты ешь/*ty yesh* | you eat | вы еди́те/*vy yeditye* | you eat |
| он ест/*on yest* | he eats | они́ едя́т/*ani yedyat* | they eat |

past tense: ел, е́ло, е́ла, е́ли

**иска́ть   to look for**

| | | | |
|---|---|---|---|
| я ищу́/*ya ishchoo* | I look for | мы и́щем/*my ishchem* | we look for |
| ты и́щешь/*ty ishchesh* | you look for | вы и́щете/*vy ishchetye* | you look for |
| он и́щет/*on ishchet* | he looks for | они́ и́щут/*ani ishchoot* | they look for |

## English-Russian Topic Vocabularies

### *Numbers* (Чи́сла/*Chisla*)

*Cardinal numbers 21–1000*

| | | | |
|---|---|---|---|
| 21 | **два́дцать оди́н**/*dvatsat adin* | 200 | **две́сти**/*dvyesti* |
| 25 | **два́дцать пять**/*dvatsat pyat* | 300 | **три́ста**/*trista* |
| 30 | **три́дцать**/*tridsat* | 400 | **четы́реста**/*chetyrista* |
| 40 | **со́рок**/*sorak* | 500 | **пятьсо́т**/*pyatsot* |
| 50 | **пятьдеся́т**/*pyatdisyat* | 600 | **шестьсо́т**/*shestsot* |
| 60 | **шестьдеся́т**/*shestdisyat* | 700 | **семьсо́т**/*syemsot* |
| 70 | **се́мьдесят**/*syemdisyat* | 800 | **восемьсо́т**/*vosyemsot* |
| 80 | **во́семьдесят**/*vosyemdisyat* | 900 | **девятьсо́т**/*dyevyatsot* |
| 90 | **девяно́сто**/*dyevyanosta* | 1000 | **ты́сяча**/*tysyacha* |
| 100 | **сто**/*sto* | | |

*Ordinal numbers 1st–20th*

| | | | |
|---|---|---|---|
| 1st | **пе́рвый**/*perviy* | 11th | **оди́ннадцатый**/*adinnatsatiy* |
| 2nd | **второ́й**/*ftaroi* | 12th | **двена́дцатый**/*dvinatsatiy* |
| 3rd | **тре́тий**/*tretiy* | 13th | **трина́дцатый**/*trinatsatiy* |
| 4th | **четвёртый**/*chetvyortiy* | 14th | **четы́рнадцатый**/*chetyrnatsatiy* |
| 5th | **пя́тый**/*pyatiy* | 15th | **пятна́дцатый**/*pitnatsatiy* |
| 6th | **шесто́й**/*shestoi* | 16th | **шестна́дцатый**/*shesnatsatiy* |
| 7th | **седьмо́й**/*syedmoi* | 17th | **семна́дцатый**/*syemnatsatiy* |
| 8th | **восьмо́й**/*vasmoi* | 18th | **восемна́дцатый**/*vosyemnatsatiy* |
| 9th | **девя́тый**/*devyatiy* | 19th | **девятна́дцатый**/*divyatnatsatiy* |
| 10th | **деся́тый**/*desyatiy* | 20th | **двадца́тый**/*dvatsatiy* |

### *The date* (Число́/*Chislo*)

| | | | |
|---|---|---|---|
| January | **янва́рь**/*yanvar* | July | **ию́ль**/*iyool* |
| February | **февра́ль**/*fevral* | August | **а́вгуст**/*avgoost* |
| March | **март**/*mart* | September | **сентя́брь**/*sentyabr* |
| April | **апре́ль**/*aprel* | October | **октя́брь**/*aktyabr* |
| May | **май**/*mai* | November | **ноя́брь**/*noyabr* |
| June | **ию́нь**/*iyoon* | December | **дека́брь**/*dekabr* |

Use the neuter ending for dates:

| | |
|---|---|
| 1st March | **пе́рвое ма́рта** |
| 5th June | **пя́тое ию́ня** |

### *Public Holidays*

| | | |
|---|---|---|
| 1 January | (**пе́рвое января́**) | New Year's Day |
| 8 March | (**восьмо́е ма́рта**) | Women's Day |
| 1 & 2 May | (**пе́рвое и второ́е ма́я**) | May Day |
| 9 May | (**девя́тое ма́я**) | Victory Day |
| 7 October | (**седьмо́е октября́**) | Constitution Day |
| 7 & 8 November | (**седьмо́е и восьмо́е ноября́**) | October Revolution Days |

# VOCABULARY

## Food

### Meat (Мясо/Myasa)

| | |
|---|---|
| beef | говя́дина/guvyadina |
| chicken | ку́рица/kuritsa |
| duck | у́тка/utka |
| goose | гусь/goos |
| lamb | бара́нина/baranina |
| pork | свини́на/svinina |
| steak | антреко́т/antrecot |
| turkey | инде́йка/indeika |
| veal | теля́тина/tilyatina |
| liver | печёнка/pichonka |
| kidneys | по́чки/pochki |

### Fish (Ры́ба/Ryba)

| | |
|---|---|
| assorted fish | ры́бная заку́ска/rybnaya zakuska |
| carp | карп/karp |
| caviare | икра́/ikra |
| cod | треска́/triska |
| crab | краб/krab |
| herring | сельдь/syeld |
| pike | щу́ка/shchooka |
| pike perch | суда́к/sudak |
| trout | форе́ль/faryel |
| salmon | сёмга/syomga лосо́сь/lasos |
| sprats | шпро́ты/shproty |
| sturgeon | осетри́на/asyetrina |

### Vegetables (О́вощи/Ovashchi)

| | |
|---|---|
| beans | фасо́ль/fasol |
| cabbage | капу́ста/kapusta |
| carrots | морко́вь/markov |
| cauliflower | цветна́я капу́ста/tsvitnaya kapusta |
| cucumber | огуре́ц/aguryets |
| mushrooms | грибы́/griby |
| onion | лук/look |
| peas | горо́х/garoxh |
| potatoes | карто́фель/kartofil |
| radish | реди́ска/rediska |
| salad | сала́т/salat |
| tomatoes | помидо́ры/pamidory |

### Fruit (Фру́кты/Frukty)

| | |
|---|---|
| apple | я́блоко/yablaka |
| banana | бана́н/banan |
| cherries | ви́шни/vishni |
| grapes | виногра́д/vinagrad |
| grapefruit | гре́йпфрут/grapefroot |
| lemon | лимо́н/limon |
| melon | ды́ня/dynya |
| orange | апельси́н/apilseen |
| peach | пе́рсик/persik |
| pear | гру́ша/grusha |
| plum | сли́ва/sliva |
| raspberry | мали́на/malina |
| strawberry | клубни́ка/kloobnika |

### Groceries (Бакале́йные това́ры/Bakalyeinye tavary)

| | |
|---|---|
| biscuits | пече́нье/pichyeni |
| butter | ма́сло/masla |
| cheese | сыр/syr |
| coffee | ко́фе/kofi |
| (without chicory) | без цико́рия/byez tsikoriya |
| cream | сли́вки/slivki (pl.) |
| flour | мука́/mooka |
| lard | жир/zhir |
| margarine | маргари́н/margarin |
| rice | рис/rees |
| sugar | са́хар/saxhar |
| tea | чай/chai |
| tinned goods | консе́рвы/kanservy |

### Car parts (Дета́ли маши́ны/Detaly mashiny)

| | |
|---|---|
| accelerator | акселера́тор/aksyelerator |
| battery | батаре́я/batereya |
| brakes | тормоза́/tarmaza |
| clutch | сцепле́ние/stsipleniye |
| engine | мото́р/mator |
| exhaust | выхлопна́я труба́/vyxhlapnaya trooba |
| headlights | фа́ры/fary |
| horn | гудо́к/goodok |
| ignition | зажига́ние/zazhiganiye |
| indicators | указа́тели поворо́та/ukazateli pavarota |
| plugs | свечи́/svechi |
| tyre | ши́на/shina |
| (steering) wheel | (рулево́е) колесо́/(rulivoye) kaliso |
| wheels | колёса/kalyosa |

# VOCABULARY

| | |
|---|---|
| windscreen wipers | **стеклоочисти́тели**/*stikla-achistitili* |
| spare parts | **запча́сти**/*zapchasti* |

## Clothes (**Оде́жда**/*Adyezhda*)

| | |
|---|---|
| bathing costume | **купа́льный костю́м**/*kupalniy kastyoom* |
| belt | **по́яс**/*poyas* |
| blouse | **блу́зка**/*bloozka* |
| boots | **сапоги́**/*sapagi* |
| bra | **ли́фчик**/*leefchik* |
| briefs | **тру́сики**/*troosiki* |
| cardigan | **шерстяно́й дже́мпер**/*sherstyanoi dzhemper* |
| coat | **пальто́**/*palto* |
| dress | **пла́тье**/*platye* |
| fur coat | **шу́ба**/*shooba* |
| gloves | **перча́тки**/*pirchatki* |
| hat | **шля́па**/*shlyapa* |
| jacket | **пиджа́к**/*pidzhak* |
| jeans | **джи́нсы**/*dzhinsy* |
| raincoat | **плащ**/*plashch* |
| scarf | **шарф**/*sharf* |
| shirt | **руба́шка**/*rubashka* |
| shoes | **ту́фли**/*toofli* |
| skirt | **ю́бка**/*yoopka* |
| socks | **носки́**/*naski* |
| stockings | **чулки́**/*choolki* |
| sweater | **сви́тер**/*sviter* |
| sweatshirt | **спорти́вный сви́тер**/*spartivniy sviter* |
| tie | **га́лстук**/*galstook* |
| tights | **колго́тки**/*kalgotki* |
| T-shirt, vest | **ма́йка**/*maika* |
| underpants | **кальсо́ны**/*kalsony* |

## Parts of the body (**Ча́сти те́ла**/*Chasti tyela*)

| | |
|---|---|
| arm | **рука́**/*rooka* |
| back | **спина́**/*spina* |
| blood | **кровь**/*krov* |
| bone | **кость**/*kost* |
| chest | **грудь**/*groot* |
| ear(s) | **у́хо, у́ши**/*ukha, ushi* |
| elbow | **ло́коть**/*lokat* |
| eye(s) | **глаз, глаза́**/*glaz, glaza* |
| face | **лицо́**/*litso* |
| finger | **па́лец**/*palyets* |
| foot | **нога́**/*naga* |
| forehead | **лоб**/*lop* |
| hair | **во́лосы**/*volasy* |

| | |
|---|---|
| hand | **рука́**/*rooka* |
| head | **голова́**/*galava* |
| knee | **коле́но**/*kalyena* |
| leg | **нога́**/*naga* |
| mouth | **рот**/*rot* |
| neck | **ше́я**/*sheya* |
| nose | **нос**/*nos* |
| shoulder | **плечо́**/*plicho* |
| stomach | **желу́док**/*zheludak* |
| throat | **го́рло**/*gorla* |
| toe | **па́лец на ноге́**/*palyets na nagye* |
| tooth | **зуб**/*zoop* |

## Toiletries (**Предме́ты туале́та**/*Predmyety twalyeta*)

| | |
|---|---|
| brush | **щётка**/*shchotka* |
| comb | **гре́бень**/*gryebin* |
| eau-de-Cologne | **одеколо́н**/*adikalon* |
| face cream | **крем для лица́**/*krem dlya litsa* |
| hand cream | **крем для рук**/*krem dlya rook* |
| nappies | **пелёнки**/*pilyonki* |
| perfume | **духи́**/*dooxhi* |
| powder | **пу́дра**/*poodra* |
| razor | **бри́тва**/*britva* |
| razor blades | **ле́звия**/*lezviya* |
| shaving cream | **крем для бритья́**/*krem dlya britya* |
| soap | **мы́ло**/*myla* |
| suntan oil | **ма́сло для зага́ра**/*masla dlya zagara* |
| tooth brush | **зубна́я щётка**/*zoobnaya shchotka* |
| toothpaste | **зубна́я па́ста**/*zoobnaya pasta* |
| shampoo | **шампу́нь**/*shampoon* |

## Jobs (**Профе́ссии**/*Prafessii*)

| | |
|---|---|
| accountant | **бухга́лтер**/*bukhgalter* |
| artist | **худо́жник**/*khudozhnik* |
| businessman | **коммерса́нт**/*kammirsant* |
| chef | **по́вар**/*povar* |
| doctor | **врач**/*vrach* |
| economist | **экономи́ст**/*ekanamist* |

# VOCABULARY

| engineer | **инжене́р/** *inzhenyer* | writer | **писа́тель, -ница/** *pisatyel, -nitsa* |
| hairdresser | **парикма́хер/** *parikmakher* | | |
| journalist | **журнали́ст/** *zhoornalist* | | |
| lawyer | **адвока́т/** *advakat* | | |
| mathematician | **матема́тик/** *matimatik* | | |
| mechanic | **меха́ник/** *mekhanik* | | |

engineer **инжене́р/** *inzhenyer*
hairdresser **парикма́хер/** *parikmakher*
journalist **журнали́ст/** *zhoornalist*
lawyer **адвока́т/** *advakat*
mathematician **матема́тик/** *matimatik*
mechanic **меха́ник/** *mekhanik*
nurse **медсестра́/** *myedsistra*
pensioner **пенсионе́р(ка)/** *pinsioner(ka)*
programmer **программи́ст/** *programmist*
salesman **продаве́ц/** *pradavyets*
saleswoman **продавщи́ца/** *prodavshitsa*
student **студе́нт(ка)/** *stoodyent(ka)*
teacher **учи́тель, –ница/** *uchityel, -nitsa*

writer **писа́тель, -ница/** *pisatyel, -nitsa*

## *Things to see* (**Достопримеча́тельности/** *Dastaprimechatelnasti*)

archaeology **археоло́гия/** *arkhealogiya*
architecture **архитекту́ра/** *arkhitektura*
art **иску́сство/** *iskusstva*
castle **за́мок/** *zamak*
cemetery **кла́дбище/** *kladbishche*
exhibition **вы́ставка/** *vystavka*
fortress **кре́пость/** *krepast*
gardens **сады́/** *sady*
monastery **монасты́рь/** *monastyr*
palace **дворе́ц/** *dvaryets*
park **парк/** *park*
ruins **разва́лины/** *razvaliny*
tomb **моги́ла/** *magila*

# Russian-English Vocabulary

**а** *a* and, but
**авиаписьмо́** *aviapismo* airmail letter
**авто́бус** *aftobus* bus
**америка́нец** *amerikanyets* (m.) American
**америка́нка** *amerikanka* (f.) American
**америка́нский/ая/ое/ие** *amerikanskiy/aya/aye/iye* (adj.) American
**англи́йский/ая/ое/ие** *angliiskiy/aya/aye/iiye* (adj.) English
**англича́нин/-ча́нка** *anglichanin/-chanka* Englishman/woman
**А́нглия** *Angliya* England
**апте́ка** *aptyeka* chemist's
**атле́тика** *atletika* athletics
**аэропо́рт** *aeroport* airport

**ба́бушка** *babushka* grandmother
**бага́ж** *bagazh* luggage
**бакале́я** *bakaleya* grocer's; groceries
**бале́т** *balyet* ballet
**банк** *bank* bank
**бар** *bar* bar
**бассе́йн для пла́вания** *bassein dlya plavaniya* swimming pool
**без** *byez* without, minus
**бе́лый/ая/ое/ые** *byely/aya/aye/ye* white
**бензи́н** *benzin* petrol
**беспоко́ить** *byespakoit* disturb; **-ся** *-sa* worry
**библиоте́ка** *bibliatyeka* library
**биле́т** *bilyet* ticket
**ближа́йший/ая/ее/ие** *blizhaishiy/aya/yeye/iye* nearest
**бли́нчик** *blinchik* pancake
**блу́зка** *bloozka* blouse
**блю́до** *blyooda* dish, course
**боли́т: у меня́ –** *balit: u minya –* my ... hurts
**боль** *bol* pain

116

# VOCABULARY

**больни́ца** *balnitsa* hospital
**бо́льше ничего́** *bolshe nichevo* nothing else
**большо́й/а́я/о́е/и́е** *balshoi/aya/oye/iye* large, big
**бу́дет** *boodyet* (there) will be; **вы бу́дете ...?** *vy booditye ...?* will you have ...?
**бу́лочка** *boolachka* roll
**бу́лочная** *boolachnaya* baker's
**бума́га** *boomaga* paper
**бума́жник** *boomazhnik* wallet
**бутербро́д** *booterbrod* sandwich
**буты́лка** *bootylka* bottle
**бюро́** *byooro* office; **– нахо́док** – *nakhodak* lost property office; **– обслу́живания** – *apsluzhivaniya* service bureau
**бы́стро** *bystra* quick(ly)
**быть** *byt* to be

**в** *v* in, at, to
**ваго́н** *vagon* carriage; **спа́льный –** *spalniy vagon* sleeping car; **– -рестора́н** – *-ristaran* dining car
**валю́та** *valyoota* (foreign) currency
**ва́нная** *vannaya* bathroom
**варе́нье** *varenye* jam
**ваш/ва́ша/ва́ше/ва́ши** *vash/vasha/vashe/vashi* (adj.) your
**вероя́тно** *verayatna* probably
**весь/вся/всё/все** *vyes/vsya/vsyo/vsye* (adj.) all
**ветчина́** *vyetchina* ham
**ве́чер** *vyecher* evening; **–ом** *–am* in the evening
**вечери́нка** *vyecherinka* party
**взять напрока́т** *vzyat naprakat* hire
**ви́деть** *vidyet* see; **я ви́жу** *ya vizhoo* I see
**вино́** *vino* wine
**винова́т/а** *vinavat/a* (adj. m/f.) sorry (guilty)
**виногра́д** *vinagrad* grapes
**витри́на** *vitrina* (shop) window
**вку́сный/ая/ое/ые** *fkoosny/aya/aye/ye* tasty
**вода́** *vada* water
**во́дка** *vodka* vodka
**возьму́: я –** *vazmoo: ya –* I'll have (take)

**вокза́л** *vakzal* station
**вон там** *von tam* over there
**вот** *vot* here's/there's, here it is etc.
**врач** *vrach* doctor
**вре́мя** *vremya* time
**всегда́** *fsikda* always
**вчера́** *fchera* yesterday
**вход** *vkhod* entrance
**вы/вас/вам/ва́ми** *vy/vas/vam/vami* you
**вы́пишите!** *vypishitye!* Write (it) out!
**высо́кий/ая/ое/ие** *vysokiy/aya/aye/iye* high
**вы́ставка** *vystavka* exhibition
**вы́ход** *vykhad* exit

**газе́та** *gazyeta* newspaper
**галере́я** *galireya* gallery
**гардеро́б** *garderob* cloakroom
**где** *gdye* where
**гид** *geed* guide
**говори́ть** *gavarit* speak
**год** *god* year; **два -а тому́ наза́д** *dva -a tamoo nazat* 2 years ago
**годи́тся: э́то –** *gaditsa: eta –* it will do
**голова́** *galava* head
**го́лодный/ая/ое/ые** *goladniy/aya/aye/ye* hungry
**го́рло** *gorla* throat
**го́род** *gorat* town
**горя́чий/ая/ее/ие** *garyachiy/aya/eye/iye* hot
**господи́н; госпожа́** *gaspadin, gaspazha* Mr; Mrs, Miss; **господа́** *gaspada* gentlemen
**гости́ница** *gastinitsa* hotel
**грибы́** *griby* mushrooms
**гру́ша** *grusha* pear

**да** *da* yes
**дава́ть** *davat* give; **да́йте!** *daitye!* give! **дава́йте** *davaitye* let's; **даю́т** *dayoot* they're doing (giving) (play etc.)
**дверь** *dver* (f.) door
**дворе́ц** *dvaryets* palace
**де́вушка** *dyevushka* girl, waitress
**дежу́рная** *dizhurnaya* corridor attendant
**деклара́ция** *diklaratsiya* declaration

# VOCABULARY

**де́лать** *dyelat* do, make;
– **сни́мки** – *snimki* take snaps
**де́ло** *dyela* business, affair; **как
дела́?** *kak dyela?* How are
things?; **по дела́м** *po dyelam* on
business
**день** *dyen* (m.) day
**де́ньги** *dyengi* (pl.) money
**дешёвый** *dishoviy* (adj.) cheap;
**деше́вле** *dishevle* cheaper
**для** *dlya* for
**до** *do* to, up to, as far as, before
**до́брый/ая/ое/ые**
*dobriy/aya/aye/ye* good
**до́лжен/должна́/должно́/должны́**
*dolzhen/dulzhna/dulzho/dulzhny*
must
**дом** *dom* house; **до́ма** *doma* at
home
**дорого́й/а́я/о́е/и́е**
*darogiy/aya/oye/iye* dear
**до свида́ния** *da svidaniya*
goodbye
**дре́вний/яя/ее/ее**
*drevniy/yaya/yeye/iye* ancient
**друг** *drook* friend (m.)
**ду́мать** *dumat* think; **я ду́маю**
*ya dumayoo* I think

**Евро́па** *Yevropa* Europe
**его́** *yevo* (acc. & gen.) him, it; his,
its
**еда́** *yeda* food
**её** *yeyo* (acc. & gen.) her, it; hers,
its
**ему́, ей** *yemoo, yei* (dat.) him, her
**есть** *yest* there is
**е́хать** *yekhat* to go (by transport)
**ещё** *yisho* still, yet; – **оди́н** – *adin*
another; – **раз** – *raz* again;
**что** – **?** *shto* – *?* what else?

**жаль** *zhal* sorry
**жа́рко** *zharka* it's hot
**жена́** *zhena* wife
**же́нский** *zhenskiy* (adj.) ladies'
**жить** *zhit* live; **я живу́** *ya zhivoo*
I live
**журна́л** *zhurnal* magazine

**за** *za* at, (+ inst.) behind
**заверни́те!** *zavirnitye!* wrap it up!
**за́втра** *zaftra* tomorrow
**заказа́ть** *zakazat* order; **я
заказа́л** *ya zakazal* I ordered

**закрыва́ться** *zakryvatsa* close
(doors, museums)
**закры́ть** *zakryt* close
**заку́ски** *zakuski* appetisers,
snacks
**заку́сочная** *zakusachnaya* snack
bar
**замеча́тельный/ая/ое/ые**
*zamichatyelniy/aya/aye/ye*
wonderful, great
**за́нят/занята́/за́нято/за́няты**
*zanyat/zanyata/zanyata/zanyaty*
occupied, engaged, taken
**заплати́те!** *zaplatitye!* pay!
**запреща́ется, запрещён**
*zaprishaetsa, zaprishon* (it's)
forbidden
**зате́м** *zatyem* then
**запра́вочная коло́нка**
*zapravachnaya kalonka* service
station
**звони́ть** *zvanit* phone
**знать** *znat* know
**зову́т: меня́** – *zavut: minya* – my
name is

**и** *i* and
**игра́ть** *igrat* play
**идти́** *ittee* go, be on (play); **я иду́**
*ya idoo* I go
**из** *iz* from, out of
**извини́те** *izvinitye* excuse me
**икра́** *ikra* caviare
**и́ли** *ili* or
**и́мя** *imya* (first) name; **и́мени**
*imeni* in the name of
**интере́сный/ая/ое/ые**
*interyesniy/aya/aye/ye*
interesting
**их** *ikh* them; their

**к** *k* to, towards
**ка́жется** *kazhitsa* it seems
**как** *kak* how
**како́й/а́я/о́е/и́е** *kakoi/aya/oye/iye*
what, which
**капу́ста** *kapusta* cabbage
**ка́рта** *karta* map
**карто́фель** *kartofil* (m.) potato
**ка́рточка** *kartachka* card, chit;
**креди́тная** – *kreditnaya* – credit
card
**ка́сса** *kassa* cash desk
**кафе́** *kafe* cafe
**квита́нция** *kvitantsiya* receipt

118

# VOCABULARY

**кино́** *kino* cinema
**кио́ск** *kiosk* kiosk
**ключ** *klyooch* key
**когда́** *kugda* when
**ко́жа** *kozha* leather
**колбаса́** *kalbasa* sausage
**коне́ц** *kanyets* end
**конве́рт** *kanvyert* envelope
**коне́чно** *kanyeshna* of course
**конфе́ты** *kanfyety* sweets
**конце́рт** *kantsert* concert
**копе́йка/копе́йки/копе́ек**
  *kapyeika/kapyeiki/kapeyek*
  kopeck(s)
**кори́чневый** *karichnyeviy* brown
**коро́бка** *karopka* box
**кото́рый/ая/ое/ые**
  *katoriy/aya/aye/ye* who, what,
  which; **– час?** *– chas?* what's the
  time?
**ко́фе** *kofi* coffee
**краси́вый/ая/ое/ые**
  *krasiviy/aya/aye/ye* beautiful,
  lovely
**кра́сный/ая/ое/ые**
  *krasniy/aya/aye/ye* red
**Крым** *Krym* Crimea
**кто** *kto* who; **– -то** *– -ta* someone
**куда́** *kooda* where to
**купа́льный костю́м** *kupalniy*
  *kastyoom* bathing costume
**купа́ться** *kupatsa* swim
**купи́ть** *kupeet* buy
**кури́ть** *kureet* smoke
**ку́рица** *kuritsa* chicken

**ле́вая (сторона́)** *lyevaya (starana)*
  left (side)
**ли** *li* interrog. particle
**лимо́н** *limon* lemon; **с -ом** *s -am*
  with lemon
**лимона́д** *limanat* lemonade
**ли́ния** *liniya* line
**литр** *litr* litre
**лифт** *lift* lift
**ло́дка** *lotka* boat
**ло́жка** *lozhka* spoon
**лу́чше** *looshe* better, best
**люби́ть** *lyoobit* love; **я люблю́**
  *ya lublyoo* I love
**лю́ди** *lyoodi* people

**мавзоле́й** *mavzolei* tomb,
  mausoleum

**ма́ленький/ая/ое/ие**
  *malinkiy/aya/aye/iye* little
**ма́рка** *marka* stamp; **5 ма́рок**
  *5 marak* 5 stamps
**ма́сло** *masla* butter
**маши́на** *mashina* car
**мёд** *myod* honey; mead
**ме́дленно** *myedlinno* slowly
**междунаро́дный** *mizhdunarodniy*
  international
**меню́** *minyoo* menu
**меня́/мне/мно́й**
  *minya/mnye/mnoi* me
**ме́сто** *myesta* place, seat
**метро́** *mitro* tube, metro
**милиционе́р** *militsianer*
  policeman
**минера́льная вода́** *mineralnaya*
  *vada* mineral water
**мину́та** *minoota* minute
**мо́жет быть** *mozhet byt* maybe
**мо́жно** *mozhna* one can, etc.
**мой/моя́/моё/мои́**
  *moi/maya/mayo/mayee* (adj.) my
**молодо́й/а́я/о́е/ы́е**
  *maladoi/aya/oye/iye* young
**молоко́** *malako* milk
**моро́женое** *marozhenaye* ice
  cream
**Москва́** *Maskva* Moscow
**мочь** *moch* be able; **я могу́** *ya*
  *magoo* I can
**мужско́й** *muzhskoi* (adj.) men's
**музе́й** *muzei* museum
**му́зыка** *muzyka* music
**мы** *my* we
**мы́ло** *myla* soap
**мя́со** *myasa* meat

**на** *na* for, to, on
**на́до** *nada* one ought, etc.
**нале́во** *nalyeva* to/on the left
**напи́ток** *napitak* drink; **напи́тки**
  *napitki* drinks
**напиши́те!** *napishitye!* Write·(it)
  down!
**напра́во** *naprava* to/on the right
**наприме́р** *naprimer* for example
**напро́тив** *naprotiv* opposite
**нас/нам/на́ми** *nas/nam/nami* us
**нахо́дится** *nakhoditsa* is situated
**начина́ться** *nachinatsa* begin (play
  etc.)

# VOCABULARY

**наш/на́ша/на́ше/на́ши**
*nash/nasha/nashe/nashi* (adj.) our
**недалеко́** *nidalyeko* not far
**неде́ля** *nidyelya* week
**нельзя́** *nilzya* one can't, etc.
**нет, не** *nyet, ni* no, not
**ничего́** *nichevo* nothing
**но** *no* but
**но́вый/ая/ое/ые** *noviy/aya/aye/ye*
new
**но́мер** *nomir* (room) number
**ночь** *noch* (f.) night
**нра́вится: мне** – *nravitsa: mnye* –
I like it
**ну́жен/нужна́/ну́жно/нужны́**
*nuzhen/nuzhna/nuzhna/nuzhny*
have or need; **мне ну́жно** *mnye*
*nuzhna* I need

**о, об** *o, ob* about
**обе́д** *abyed* lunch
**обме́н де́нег** *abmyen dyenek*
currency exchange
**обменя́ть** *abminyat* exchange
**обра́тно** *abratna* back
**о́вощи** *ovashchi* vegetables
**огуре́ц** *aguryets* cucumber
**оде́жда** *adyezhda* clothes
**одея́ло** *adiyalo* blanket
**окно́** *akno* window
**омле́т** *amlyet* omelet
**он, она́, оно́, они́** *on, ana, ano,
ani* he (it), she (it), it, they
**о́пера** *opira* opera
**орке́стр** *arkestr* orchestra
**осетри́на** *asyetrina* sturgeon
**оста́вить** *astavit* leave, park (car)
**остано́вка** *astanofka* (bus etc.)
stop
**от** *ot* from
**отвеча́ть** *atvichat* answer
**отде́л** *atdyel* department
**отдыха́ть** *atdykhat* rest, go on
holiday
**открыва́ться** *atkryvatsa* open
(museums etc.)
**откры́тка** *atkrytka* postcard
**отли́чно!** *atlichna!* excellent!
**отправле́ние** *atpravleniye*
departure
**отправля́ться** *atpravlyatsa* depart,
set off
**о́тпуск** *otpusk* holiday, leave; **в –е**

*v –ye* on holiday
**отходи́ть** *atkhadit* leave, go away
**о́чень** *ochin* very
**оши́бка** *ashipka* mistake

**па́мятник** *pamyatnik* monument
**па́спорт** *paspart* passport
**папиро́са** *papirosa* Russian
cigarette
**пе́рвый/ая/ое/ые**
*pyerviy/aya/aye/ye* first
**пе́ред** *piryed* before
**переса́дка** *pirisatka* connection,
transfer **де́лать переса́дку**
*dyelat pirisatkoo* change (train
etc.)
**пи́во** *piva* beer
**пирожки́** *pirazhki* pies
**пиро́жное** *pirozhnaye* pastry;
fancy cake
**писа́ть** *pisat* write
**письмо́** *pismo* letter
**пить** *peet* drink
**пла́вать** *plavat* swim
**пласти́нка** *plastinka* record
**плати́ть** *platit* pay
**плато́к** *platok* headscarf
**пла́тье** *platye* dress
**платфо́рма** *platforma* platform
**плёнка** *plyonka* film
**плохо́й/а́я/о́е/и́е**
*ploxhoy/aya/oye/iye* bad **мне
пло́хо** *mnye ploxha* I feel ill
**пло́щадь** *ploshchad* (f.) square
**пляж** *plyazh* beach
**по** *po* along: **– -англи́йски**
– *-angliiski* in English;
**– -ру́сски** – *-russki* in Russian
**повтори́те!** *paftaritye!* repeat!
**пого́да** *pagoda* weather
**пода́рки** *padarki* gifts
**подожди́те!** *padazhditye!* wait!
**подру́га** *padruga* friend (f.)
**поду́шка** *padushka* pillow
**подхо́дит: э́то вам – ?** *padkhodit:
eta vam – ?* Does that suit you?
**по́езд** *poyezd* train
**пойти́ (на бале́т)** *paeetee (na
balyet)* go (to the ballet)
**пойдём(те)** *paidyom(ti)* let's go
**пожа́луйста** *pazhalasta* please,
don't mention it
**покажи́те!** *pokazhitye!* show!

# VOCABULARY

**полови́на** *palavina* half
**полоте́нце** *palatentse* towel
**поме́рить** *pamyerit* measure
**помидо́ры** *pamidory* tomatoes
**понима́ть** *panimat* understand;
  **я понима́ю** *ya panimayoo*
  I understand
**пора́** *para* it's time
**порекоменду́ете: что вы – ?**
  *porikamendooitye: shto vy – ?*
  What do you recommend?;
  **я порекоменду́ю** *ya*
  *porikamenduyoo* I recommend
**посла́ть** *paslat* send
**после́дний/яя/ее/ие**
  *pasledniy/yaya/yeye/iye* last
**посета́ь** *pasyetat* visit
**по́сле** *posli* after
**посмотре́ть** *pasmatryet* look at,
  see
**посы́лка** *pasylka* parcel
**потеря́ть** *patyeryat* lose
**пото́м** *patom* then
**по́чта** *pochta* post office
**пра́вая (сторона́)** *pravaya*
  *(starana)* right (side)
**пра́вда** *pravda* true, truth
**прекра́сный/ая/ое/ые**
  *prekrasniy/aya/aye/ye* fine,
  lovely
**прибы́тие** *pribytiye* arrival
**приходи́ть: мы придём**
  *prikhodit: my pridyom* come,
  arrive: we'll come
**приноси́ть: принесу́,**
  **принеси́те!** *prinasit: prinisoo,*
  *prinisitye!* bring: I bring, bring!
**прия́тный/ая/ое/ые**
  *priyatniy/aya/aye/ye* nice,
  pleasant
**прода́жа** *pradazha* sale; **про́даны**
  *prodany* (pl.) sold
**прое́хать** *prayekhat* get to (by
  transport)
**пройти́** *praeetye* get to (on foot)
**про́пуск** *propusk* (hotel) pass
**проси́ть** *prasit* ask, beg; **я прошу́**
  **вас** *ya prashoo vas* I ask/beg
  you; **вас про́сят** *vas prosyat*
  you're wanted
**прости́те** *prastitye* forgive/excuse
  me
**про́сто** *prosta* simply, just;
  **– пре́лесть** *– prilyest* simply

delightful
**прямо́й** *pryamoi* (adj.) direct;
  **пря́мо** *pryama* straight on
**путь** *poot* (m.) way, trip, path
**путеводи́тель** *pootivadityel* (m.)
  guidebook
**пье́са** *pyesa* play

**рабо́тать** *rabotat* work
**рад/ра́да/ра́ды** *rad/rada/rady*
  (m., f., pl.) glad, pleased (to
  meet you)
**раз** *raz* time; **три -а** *tree -a* three
  times
**разгово́р** *razgavor* conversation
**разме́н, разменя́ть** *razmyen,*
  *razminyat* change, exchange
**разме́р** *razmer* size
**расписа́ние** *raspisaniye* timetable
**распиши́тесь!** *raspishityes!* sign!
**рестора́н** *ristaran* restaurant
**рис** *rees* rice
**родили́сь: вы –** *radilis: vy –* you
  were born
**ро́зовый/ая/ое/ые**
  *rozaviy/aya/aye/ye* pink, rosé
**Росси́я** *Rassiya* Russia
**рот** *rot* mouth
**руба́шка** *rubashka* shirt
**рубль/рубли́/рубля́/рубле́й**
  *rubl/rubli/rublya/rublyei* rouble
**ру́сский/ая/ое/ие**
  *russkiy/aya/aye/iye* (adj.) Russian
**ры́ба** *ryba* fish
**ряд** *ryad* row
**ря́дом** *ryadam* next to, near

**с, со** *s, so* with, from
**сади́тесь!** *sadityes!* sit down!
**сала́т** *salat* salad
**самова́р** *samavar* samovar
**самолёт** *samalyot* aeroplane
**сапоги́** *sapagi* boots
**са́хар** *sakhar* sugar
**светофо́р** *svyetafor* traffic lights
**сви́тер** *sviter* sweater
**свобо́дно** *svabodno* (it's) free,
  vacant
**сда́ча** *sdacha* change
**сего́дня** *sivodnya* today; **–шний**
  *–shniy* (adj.) today's
**сейча́с** *syichas* at once, straight
  away
**сельдь** *syeld* (f.) herring

# VOCABULARY

**сéрдце** *serdtse* heart
**серéдина** *siridina* middle
**сигáра** *sigara* cigar
**сигарéта** *sigareta* cigarette
**сидéть** *seedyet* sit, suit (clothes)
**симпатúчный/ая/ое/ые**
*simpatichniy/aya/aye/ye* nice,
pleasant (person)
**сúний/яя/ее/ие**
*siniy/yaya/yeye/iye* blue
**скажúте!** *skazhitye!* say! **вы**
**скáжете мне?** *vy skazhitye*
*mnye?* Will you tell me?
**скóлько** *skolka* how much/many
**слáдкое** *sladkoye* dessert, sweet
**слéдующий/ая/ее/ие**
*sleduyooshchiy/aya/eye/iye* next,
following
**слúшком** *slishkam* too
**слýшать** *slushat* listen; **слýшаю**
*slushayoo* I'm listening
**смотрúте!** *smatritye!* look!
**сметáна** *smitana* sour cream
**собóр** *sabor* cathedral
**совéтский/ая/ое/ие**
*savyetskiy/aya/aye/iye* (adj.)
Soviet
**совсéм** *savsyem* quite; **– не –** *ni*
not at all
**соглáсны** *saglasny* (pl.) agreed
**сожалéнию: к** *sazhalyeniyoo: k*
unfortunately
**сок** *sok* juice
**сóлнце** *solntsi* sun; **сóлнечный**
*solnichniy* (adj.) sun
**сосúска** *sasiska* sausage
**спасúбо** *spaseeba* thank you
**спервá** *spirva* at first
**спокóйный/ая/ое/ые**
*spakoiniy/aya/aye/ye* calm,
peaceful
**спортúвный/ая/ое/ые**
*spartivniy/aya/aye/ye* (adj.)
sports
**спрáвочное бюрó**
*spravachnaye byooro*
information office
**срáзу** *srazoo* at once
**стакáн** *stakan* glass
**стáнция** *stantsiya* station
**стáрый/ая/ое/ые**
*stariy/aya/aye/ye* old
**стóит, стóят** *stoit, stoyat* costs, cost
**стол** *stol* table

**столúца** *stalitsa* capital
**столóвая** *stalovaya* dining room,
snack bar
**сторонá** *starana* side
**стоянка таксú** *stayanka taksi* taxi
rank
**стыдно** *stydna* ashamed
**сýмка** *sumka* bag; **сýмочка**
*sumachka* handbag
**сходúть** *skhadit* get out (of
vehicle)
**сюдá** *syooda* here (hither)
**сухóй/áя/óе/úе**
*sukhoi/aya/oye/iye* dry
**сыр** *syr* cheese
**схéма** *skhema* diagram, map
**счёт** *sschot* account, bill, abacus

**табáк** *tabak* tobacconist's
**тáкже** *takzhe* also
**таксú** *taksi* taxi
**талóн(ы)** *talon(y)* voucher(s)
**там** *tam* there
**теáтр** *tiatr* theatre
**телефóн** *tilifon* phone
**тепéрь** *tipyer* now
**товáрищ** *tavarisch* comrade
**тогдá** *tugda* then
**тóже** *tozhe* also, too
**тóлько** *tolka* only
**тóчно** *tochna* precisely
**тот/та/то/те** *tot/ta/to/tye* (adj.) this,
these
**трамвáй** *tramvai* tram
**троллéйбус** *trallyeibus* trolleybus
**туалéт** *twalyet* toilet
**тудá** *tooda* there (thither)
**ты/тебя/тебé/тобóй**
*ty/tibya/tibye/taboi* you (fam.)

**у** *u* in the possession of, at the
home of **– меня –** *minya* I have
**увúдите** *uviditye* you will see
**ýгол: на углý** *ugal: na ugloo* at the
corner
**угóдно: что вам – ?** *ugodna: shto*
*vam – ?* What would you like?
**удивúтельно** *udivityelna* it's
wonderful
**удовóльствие: с –м** *udavolstviye:*
*s –m* with pleasure
**ужáсно** *uzhasna* it's dreadful
**ýжин** *uzhin* supper
**ýлица** *ulitsa* street

122

# VOCABULARY

**у́тро** *utra* morning; **–м** *–m* in the morning
**учи́тель** *uchityel* teacher

**хлеб** *khlyep* bread
**хоккéй** *khakkei* (ice) hockey
**холóдный/ая/ое/ые**
  *khalodniy/aya/aye/ye* cold
**хорóший/ая/ее/ие**
  *kharoshiy/aya/eye/iye* good
  **хорошó** *kharasho* fine, OK
**хóтеть** *khotet* want; **я хочý** *ya khachoo* I want; **хоти́те?**
  *khatitye?* Do you want?
**хóчется: мне** – *khochitsa: mnye* –
  I feel like

**фами́лия** *familiya* surname
**фильм** *film* film
**фотоаппарáт** *fotaapparat* camera
**фотографи́ровать** *fatagrafiravat*
  to photograph
**фрýкты** *frukty* (pl.) fruit;
  **фруктóвый** *fruktoviy* (adj.) fruit
**фунт, фýнты** *funt, funty* pound,
  pounds
**футбóл** *footbol* football

**цвет** *tsvet* colour
**с цвéтами** *s tsvetami* with flowers
**ценá** *tsena* price
**центр** *tsentr* centre; **– гóрода**
  – *gorada* town centre
  **центрáльный** *tsentralniy* (adj.)
  central
**цéрковь** *tserkof* (f.) church
**цирк** *tsirk* circus

**чай** *chai* tea

**час** *chas* hour, o'clock; **-ы́** *-y*
  (pl.) watch
**чáшка** *chashka* cup
**чек** *chek* receipt
**человéк** *chelavyek* person
**чемодáн** *chemadan* suitcase
**чемпионáт** *chempionat*
  championship
**чéрез** *cheryez* after
**чёрный/ая/ое/ые**
  *chorniy/aya/aye/ye* black
**что** *shto* what, that; **– ещё** – *yisho*
  anything else; **– -нибудь (от)** –
  *-niboot (ot)* something (for)
**чýвствовать: чýвствую себя́**
  *choostvavat: choostvuyoo sibya*
  I feel
**чудéсно** *chudyesna* it's wonderful

**шипýчий/ая/ее/ие**
  *shipoochiy/aya/yeye/iye*
  sparkling
**шоколáд** *shakalat* chocolate;
  **шоколáдный** *shakaladniy* (adj.)
  chocolate

**экскýрсия** *ekskursiya* excursion
**этáж** *etazh* floor, storey
**э́то** *eta* it's
**э́тот/э́та/э́то/э́ти** *etat/eta/eta/eti*
  (adj.) this, these

**я** *ya* I
**я́блоко** *yablako* apple
**яи́чница** *yaichnitsa* fried eggs
**яйцó, я́йца** *yaitso, yaitsa* egg,
  eggs
**язы́к** *yazyk* language